New England Snow Country:

701 Ways to Enjoy Winter Whether You Ski or Not

by
Barbara Radcliffe Rogers
&
Stillman Rogers

New England Snow Country:

701 Ways to Enjoy Winter Whether You Ski or Not

by
Barbara Radcliffe Rogers
&
Stillman Rogers

Williams Hill Publishing
Grafton, New Hampshire

This publication is designed to provide accurate and authoritative information in regard to the subject matter covered. The prices and information listed in this guidebook were confirmed at press time. We recommend you call the establishments listed to obtain current information before traveling, as neither publisher nor writer can be held accountable for any changes.

First Edition

Printed in the United States of America

10 9 8 7 6 5 4 3 2 1

Publisher's Cataloging-in-Publication

Rogers, Barbara Radcliffe.
    New England snow country : 701 ways to enjoy
    winter whether you ski or not / by Barbara Radcliffe
    Rogers & Stillman Rogers. — 1st ed.
        p. cm.
        Includes index.
            LCCN: 99-67041
            ISBN: 0-9652502-6-1

        1. Winter sports—Massachusetts—Guidebooks.
    2. Winter sports—Vermont—Guidebooks. 3. Winter
    sports—New Hampshire—Guidebooks. 4. Winter
    sports—Maine—Guidebooks. 5. Winter resorts—
    Massachusetts—Guidebooks. 6. Winter resorts—
    Vermont—Guidebooks. 7. Winter resorts—New Hampshire—
    Guidebooks. 8. Winter resorts—Maine—Guidebooks.
    9. Massachusetts—Guidebooks. 10. Vermont—Guidebooks.
    11. New Hampshire— Guidebooks. 12. Maine—Guidebooks.
    I. Rogers, Stillman, 1939- II. Title.

    GV840.7.N35R64 1999   796.9'0974
                                           QBI99-1467

Published by Williams Hill Publishing
RR 1 Box 1234
Grafton NH 03240
603-523-7877
www.williamshillpub.com

Cover photographs courtesy of State of NH Office of Travel and Tourism Development, from left to right: Brooks Dodge; OTTD; Bob Grant; William Johnson.

To Charles, who taught me to ski, and to Shirley, the Vermonter he married — Barbara

To Paul Flayhan, with whom I shared my first hair-raising runs from the top of the mountain — Tim

TABLE OF CONTENTS

A FEW WORDS OF THANKS

We didn't set out to research and write this book in the usual way. Instead, we've simply written down those things we've always enjoyed doing in the longest season of the year. We've had a long time to collect the adventures and experiences in this book, since we have lived most of our lives in New England, and when we lived elsewhere we spent a lot of our winter weekends flying home to ski or snowshoe or watch the fire flicker as the wind howled outside. In the course of all these years we have shared our New England winters with a lot of people, and a lot of people have shared their favorite places with us.

We'd like to mention a few of them. First, our ski buddies: Charles Radcliffe, Paul Flayhan, Pat Hanson, Carole Bazely, Annie Grubb MacBurney, Dick Martin, Bob Emond, Ron Weeden, John Arnold, Larry Pletcher, Eric Burt, Frank and Maria Sibley, and Julie, Lura, Cherie and Briana Rogers. We've shared as many laughs with them as we have miles of trails.

Barbara Thomke, Sara Widness, Kathe Dillman, Nancy Marshall, Dick Hamilton, Mike Duprey, Glen Faria, Bill De Sousa, Scott Peterson, Pam Cruikshank, Susan Logan, Marie Pacetta, Elizabeth Elliot, Halley McEvoy, Laura Arneson, Myra Foster, Patrick McMorrow and Peter Mackey have all helped us by suggesting places to go and by helping us get there. And to our many hosts—those innkeepers who welcomed and warmed us after a day in the snow and the chefs whose fine meals kept us fueled—our fondest thanks. New England's legendary (but far from mythical) hospitality is what winter here is all about.

INTRODUCTION

We both love to ski. But not every day, and not in all kinds of weather, or on all the generous variety of surface conditions a New England winter can provide. There is life beyond the slopes, after the slopes, and instead of the slopes, as well as on the slopes; skiing is a great excuse to come to northern New England in the winter, but it's not the only reason.

Whether you are a fanatical skier, an occasional skier, or one of the vast number of intelligent humans who simply don't enjoy flinging themselves off the top of a slippery mountain with waxed sticks on their feet, read on. This book is for all of you.

First of all, skiers will find the details, deals and delights of northern New England's downhill areas, from the mega-resorts like Killington to some tiny places where you can spend a day skiing well-maintained trails with the locals, and never wait in line. You'll also learn which ski areas have the best trails for the particular way you like to ski. Some areas are good for both experts and novices, others favor a particular level of skill. With this book in hand, you'll be able to pick the best one for you and for those who ski with you.

Although the state tourist offices are reluctant to admit it, there are days when skiing is almost impossible. The ubiquitous January thaw can occur anytime from December to March, and with it can come the driving rain that turns slopes the consistency of French sorbet. Or the opposite can happen, a surfeit of riches in the form of a blizzard so severe that just trying to get to the slopes—or survive on them—is just plain foolhardy. Most skiers cross their fingers that either event occurs on Sunday, so they can honestly call in on Monday morning (just before they head to the freshly blanketed slopes) and say they've been snowbound and will be back on Tuesday.

The purpose of this book is to dispel the myth that the only way to enjoy a New England winter is to ski. Skiing is one of the things you can do here between Thanksgiving and Easter, but not the only one. Some people never ski at all, others ski once in a while (we admit to being among these fair-weather skiers) and even those who ski whenever they can sneak off to the slopes, occasionally enjoy other pastimes. This book is for those who don't ski at all, those who ski sometimes, and those who must eventually leave the slopes because the lifts have stopped running. It's even for those who go to Key West for the winter, in hopes they'll read it and see what they're missing.

We have not attempted to cover all of New England, nor even all of its northern regions. There is simply too much to do for us to fit it all into one book. Instead we have confined ourselves just to the activities that are close to the major ski regions. Of course the activities that take place off the slopes aren't the only places that remain open all winter: you can curl up in front of a fire and watch the waves crash on our rocky coast in January or plan a week of lively theater, music and dining adventures in Providence or Boston (or in Portsmouth or Portland) any time during the winter. This book, however, describes the winter pleasures of the regions we New Englanders know as "Snow Country."

Do you have to like winter to enjoy it? Not really, but it helps. A sleigh ride through the frozen landscape is more fun if you find trees laden with fresh snow beautiful. This book includes many different ways of enjoying winter, and not all of them are outdoors. In the pages that follow, you'll find as many ways to enjoy northern New England's winter indoors as outdoors. Visiting museums and historic places when they are uncrowded, shopping for antiques, visiting artists in their studios to watch them create a delicately blown wine glass or a quilt, learning new cooking techniques from the chef at a country inn, retreating to a spa for an herbal body wrap, making your own balsam wreath, nibbling on scones and cream at tea time, riding a vintage train, listening to jazz, admiring a Monet, all these activities are available to winter travelers in the North Country.

The facilities of the ski resorts themselves are open to

non-skiers, who have the entire day to enjoy them in peace and quiet, while everyone else is on the slopes. The sports and fitness facilities, swimming pools, spas, and other off-slope attractions that are offered by ski resorts go largely unused until about five in the afternoon.

We hope that readers will use this book to plan winter vacations for both skiers and non-skiers. The skier in the family can choose slopes and trails while the non-skier plans how to spend the day. The après ski, lodging and dining information will be useful to everyone.

SOME WINTER ACTIVITIES IN THIS BOOK

DOWNHILL SKIING

Whether you prefer hair-raising terrain, glades, bunny slopes, or gentle scenic trails, you'll find them here. Descriptions include such details as a resort's facilities, its suitability for skiers of different skills, the length of lift lines, the quality of their grooming, and the exposure direction. You'll know where the snow lasts the longest into spring and which trails to avoid if the wind is from the north. Base-lodge facilities, such as rentals, child care, ski school and even where to find the best chili, are included. For more information on skiing, contact the tourism office of each state, listed in the introduction to each state.

SNOWBOARDING

No longer the domain of a few crazy teenagers, boarding is serious sport. In Vermont, where it was invented—at Stratton Mountain—it gets special attention. Suicide Six, a small ski area that's far more benign than its name, specializes in teaching adults to ride boards, while Killington holds weeklong boarding clinics. Smugglers Notch has a special area for teaching children to board. A few areas, including Mad River Glen in Waitsfield, Vermont, do not allow them while others have special areas for boarders and a number have half-pipe runs. Look for boarding information with downhill skiing, since they share the slopes and trails at most resorts and the information is applicable to both. At the areas especially known for their boarding facilities, there's a separate section that follows downhill skiing.

CROSS-COUNTRY SKIING

If your taste in trails runs more to horizontal than to vertical, check each chapter for the best Nordic centers and the ungroomed trails of nature reserves and parks. You'll find wilderness areas, in-town trails, level golf-course routes and more challenging woodland trails along mountainsides. When you're skiing in remote or wilderness areas, go in groups or at least pairs, and let someone know where you plan to go and when you will return, in case you run into problems. Winter in New England is filled with surprises, including un-predicted blizzards that seem to sweep in out of nowhere. If you are hurt or have damaged equipment far from a road, it's comforting to know that someone will be looking for you.

SNOWSHOEING

For those who enjoy exploring the woods and fields in the winter, but prefer to do it with footgear less slippery than skis, snowshoeing may be the answer. Basic walking skills are all that's necessary to become comfortable on snowshoes. Although this sport has recently taken off, it was a popular method of winter transportation in the mid-1800s, when New England Outing Club members would gather for snowshoe tramps. At least one ski area, you can ride to the top on the lift and snowshoe the scenic mountaintop. The same winter woods precautions that apply to Nordic skiers are also wise for snowshoe travelers: always let someone know where you will be and when you expect to return.

In Stowe, Vermont, the Tubbs Snowshoe Company has developed a new shoe design to make walking even easier, along with a new step-in binding. A good pair of commercially-made snowshoes will cost about $100, but you can also rent them from many resorts and winter sports outfitters. Some inns keep several pairs for guests' use. In New Hampshire's White Mountains, at least two snowshoe makers still craft handmade snowshoes the old-fashioned way at costs that are close to the machine-manufactured ones.

SNOWMOBILES

Access to the more remote wilderness areas in New England Snow Country is difficult, but snow machines make these wild places available. Vermont alone has over 3,000 miles of groomed snowmobile trails that are well-mapped and patrolled. The longest suspension bridge for snowmobiles in America has recently been completed to span a deep gorge near Waterbury.

The Vermont Association of Snow Travelers (VAST) maintains these trails through its more than 150 local clubs. Other states have similar groups. To find out more about the club near your winter destination in Vermont, contact the VAST state headquarters at P.O. Box 839, Montpelier, VT 05601; 802-229-0005. In Maine, contact the Maine Snowmobile Association, P.O. Box 77, Augusta, ME 04330; 207-622-6983. The New Hampshire Snowmobile Association is at P.O. Box 38, Concord, NH 03301; 603-224-8906.

ICE SKATING

A skating pond can mean anything from one the fire department keeps cleared of snow and floods periodically for local kids to an elegant landscaped pond with an arched bridge spanning its middle, wooden benches around its edge and a bonfire on an island. Or it can be a floodlit rink with a comfortable glass-walled lounge at one end, such as the one at Great Glen Trails at the foot of Mount Washington.

SLEIGH RIDES

A ride over frozen meadows is the most fun at night, and is especially beautiful during a full moon. It's a romantic adventure for two in a one-horse sleigh straight out of

Currier and Ives, or rollicking fun for the whole family in a hay-filled wagon-style sleigh behind a team of English Shires or Percherons. Sleigh rides are almost always followed by hot cocoa or mulled cider to warm up.

DOG SLEDDING
Dogsled races are held throughout snow country, and a few kennel-owners will take guests either for short rides or on longer trips into the backcountry, where they can learn the art of mushing. For information and the names of outfitters throughout New England, contact New England Sled Dog Club, 206 Chapin Road, Essex Junction, VT 05452; 802-879-6582.

ICE FISHING
This is not a sport for everyone, but it's very popular in northern New England. As soon as the ice is safe, you'll see convoys of these funny little shacks—known as bobhouses—bouncing along on trailers on their way to the lake to create temporary villages dotting the ice. Unfortunately for travelers, very few places either rent bobhouses or have the facilities to take people ice fishing. The only such program we could find was in Stowe, Vermont.

SLEDDING AND TOBOGGANING
These are rarely organized sports, and although a few towns set aside a particular hill for the kids, these winter activities tend to be spontaneous. Kids have a way of finding the good sledding hills, but if you don't see one in your travels, ask your innkeeper.

Mount Snow sets aside one trail for sledding each evening, and Smugglers Notch has a hill reserved just for sleds, but in most places you just join the locals on someone's pasture.

New to New England, but long used in Finland and other Arctic regions, kicksleds (picture an old-fashioned scooter with runners instead of wheels) are available for rent at Great Glen Trails in Pinkham Notch, New Hampshire. We personally hope these will catch on, since they are fun, safe and very practical. If you plan to sled, it's a good idea to bring your own or plan to buy one, since very few places have them available to rent.

WINTER CAMPING AND IGLOO BUILDING

Groups such as the Appalachian Mountain Club offer weekend programs and trips, where participants can learn how to travel safely in the winter, set up a camp in the snow, and even build comfortable shelters in the winter woods. Other groups have cabins or shelters which skiers and winter campers may use. Igloo-building is featured at some winter festivals, and at a special day-long program at the Montshire Museum in Norwich, Vermont.

MAPLE SUGARING

During March and April, you will see steam rising from small sugarhouses on farms all over northern New England, but some of these have museums, tours or programs as well as shops that welcome visitors.

For a list of Vermont sugar houses that welcome guests or offer tours and sugar-on-snow parties, contact the Vermont Department of Agriculture, 116 State Street, Drawer 20, Montpelier, VT 05620; 802-828-2416.

For a New Hampshire list, contact the New Hampshire Maple Producers Association, 28 Peabody Row, Dept. G, Londonderry, NH 03053; 603-267-7070.

Massachusetts sugarhouses are listed in a brochure produced by the Massachusetts Maple Producers Association, Watson-Spruce Corner Road, Ashfield, MA 01330; 413-628-3912.

Maine celebrates Maple Sunday the last weekend in March, with events and open houses at many sugarbushes. For a list of those participating, as well as those that welcome visitors at other times, contact the Maine Department of Agriculture's Marketing Development Division, State House Station 28, Augusta, ME 04333; 207-287-7636.

CHURCH, GAME AND FIREHOUSE SUPPERS

A few of these are annual events, and listed under the appropriate region, but more often they are advertised in local free newspapers and by signs in the local general store. Keep an eye out for the "Bean Supper Tonight" signs that pop up in the snowbanks in front of churches, fire stations and town halls. These are not only inexpensive hearty meals, but they are a wonderful way to meet local people and learn about an area. Seating is usually at long tables, and the conversation informal. If you see a game supper advertised, don't miss the chance to sample some of the local roadkill. It's okay, state Fish and Game Departments quick-freeze the meat and make it available to local fire departments for fund-raising suppers.

IN CASE YOU WERE WONDERING...

Northern New England and the people who live there have their own peculiarities, due in part to the long winters they must endure. Here is a primer on a few of them:

COVERED BRIDGES

We've read all sorts of hokum about why New Englanders built covered bridges, including one that suggested that early Yankees didn't know how to build anything except barns, so they adapted the barn to help them cross rivers. *Sure.* First, they are not peculiar to New England. We've traveled through bridges that look very much the same in Switzerland and alpine Italy. New Brunswick, in Canada, has a number, including the longest one in the world. Current literature has it that some county in the Midwest has a few, too.

Most of the remaining ones are in New England, primarily in New Hampshire and Vermont, where they are treasured, and many are still in daily use (including the one we cross on our way to the Post Office every day).

Their purpose was not to keep snow off the road

surface; it actually had to be shoveled onto the bridges so sleighs could cross them. The roof was to keep the snow from piling up and causing the bridge timbers to collapse from the weight. The sloping roof helped snow to slide off. At least three covered railroad bridges remain; the Fisher Bridge in Wolcott, Vermont, north of Stowe, is the only covered railroad bridge in America still in use on a regular line. Between Claremont and Newport, New Hampshire, you can snowshoe on a trail that passes through two retired rail bridges (see *Mount Sunapee*).

Bridge "collecting" is a favorite pastime, even for natives. Several towns, including Montgomery, Vermont, give out little maps to help you locate them. Most are on year-round roads, so a bridge tour with your camera is a nice excursion on a sunny afternoon. Expect to get lost a few times, since we don't litter our roadsides with signs, and the snowbanks cover the ones we do put there.

WEATHER TALK

Probably the most common winter activity here, the first thing you should know is that it's not so much a matter of complaining, since that would indicate wimpiness we would never admit to. It's more of a can-you-top-this game. Subtle, with real old Yankees it involves a double one-upmanship—bragging is also unYankee—involving a delicate blend of what time they got up in the morning and the severity of the weather. It begins with "When I looked out after breakfast at quarter after five, it was only 20 below." Note that the speaker has left room there. The reply will be something like: "Must've warmed up quite a bit, then, since I noticed it at quarter til." This kind of conversation is getting harder to find, so listen sharp. Best place is in the kitchen at a church supper. By the way, pipes don't freeze here, they *ketch*. The past tense is *ketched*, as in "My pipes *ketched* couple of nights ago."

ABOUT THE MATTER OF AFRICANS...

Don't be alarmed or surprised if your hostess cheerily assures you that there's an African in your room in case it gets chilly in the evening. Or suggests you take one on a sleigh ride with you to keep your legs warm. Especially in the far north, those crocheted mini-blankets you find over the backs of chairs are called Africans. *You* may call them afghans, but a lot of people don't. We mean no offense to anyone.

Don't expect to hear this in a gussied-up Manchester inn—they're all run by people from Connecticut who call them "throws." But in your B&B in the Northeast Kingdom, be prepared to snuggle up with an African. You'll find them quite cozy.

Museums

Small historical museums in the North Country tend to close in the winter. There are several reasons: the high cost of heating, the relative scarcity of passing tourists and the difficulty of getting docents after the retired population has moved south for the season. It's not as though they are discriminating against winter tourists, but many of these little historical society buildings have little or no source of heat. I would not wish to sit there on a blustery Sunday afternoon waiting for the stray tourist to turn up.

But if you are really interested in seeing one of these, someone will usually be able to open them up and take you through. Sometimes there is a phone number on the sign. If there is no clue at the building, ask a) your innkeeper, b) the general storekeeper c) the local librarian. Sometimes these museums are upstairs in the library, as in Waterbury, Vermont, in which case they are open during library hours. Take cheer: tourists even have trouble finding little local museums to be open in the summer. We know of one that is open only the first Tuesdays in July and August.

MASSACHUSETTS: THE BERKSHIRES

Western Massachusetts is marked by deeply rolling countryside and the Berkshire Mountains, the southernmost range in New England. Tourism began with the "summer people." A century ago, Lenox was the darling of society's upper crust; the Vanderbilts, Carnegies and their intimates built mansions there. Stockbridge was almost as fashionable, with its share of mansions. Pittsfield, to the north, has the more down-to-earth feel of a mill town, and budget-minded vacationers are more likely to stay there than in Lenox or Stockbridge.

Cultural life in the Berkshires is stimulated, although not dominated by the presence of Williams College in its midst. Their theater program is well-known, and the arts environment there is quite strong. But the arts community, attracted by the Tanglewood Music Festival, Jacob's Pillow, summer theater festivals, and a major art museum, extends far beyond the college, even in the winter. Music is sure to play a part in any gathering or festivity in the area, at any time of year.

Contact: Berkshire Hills Visitors Bureau, Berkshire Common, Pittsfield, MA 01201; 413-443-9186 or 800-237-5747. Skiers should ask for the annual *Massachusetts Ski Guide* by calling 800-227-MASS. For ski conditions, call 413-499-7669.

DOWNHILL SKIING AND BOARDING

Why, you may ask, do we mention small ski areas in the Berkshires when there are so many larger ones only a bit farther north?

Because the attraction of these areas is not their soaring altitude or mega-slopes, but the fact that so many small, attractive ski resorts are located so close to each other in a pleasant area that's so much closer to the East Coast cities than are the major ski capitals in New England Snow Country.

No one ski area predominates, although Jiminy Peak and Brodie offer the greatest combination of lifts, trails, base-to-summit altitude and length of trails. Jiminy has challenging trails, nearly half of which are for expert skiers. We have not included areas where the longest trail is under 1.5 miles.

The major areas are **Berkshire East** on South River Road in Charlemont (413-339-6617), **Bousquet** on Tamarack Road in Pittsfield (413-442-8316), **Brodie** on Route 7 in New Ashford (413-443-4752), **Butternut** on Route 23 in Great Barrington (413-528-2000), **Catamount** on Route 23 in South Egremont (413-528-1262), and **Jiminy Peak** on Corey Road in Hancock (413-738-5500). All have snowmaking on more than 90% of the trails, and there's a good mix of terrain for various abilities.

The longest trail on any of them is two miles and *vertical drop* is not a strong term in their vocabularies. But they offer a family-friendly atmosphere, lower prices and shorter lift lines, although short runs mean you will be in line more often. Expert skiers may find a thrill or two, but will probably be happier on the taller, steeper mountains farther north.

Ski season usually begins a little later and ends earlier in the Berkshires than in the Green Mountains and White Mountains, partly because the Berkshires are farther south, and partly because of their lower altitude. Snowmaking, which depends on cold nights, is less effective and natural snow cover lighter, but while that affects the length of the season, it doesn't mean that ski conditions are inferior.

The Berkshire ski areas have learned to make the best of their season, and the grooming at Jiminy Peak, for example, is among the finest in New England.

CROSS-COUNTRY SKIING

Cross-country heaven, the Berkshires have facilities in the downhill ski areas of **Brodie,** on Route 7 in New Ashford (413-443-4752), **Butternut** on Route 23 in Great Barrington (413-528-2000) and **Otis Ridge** (413-269-4444), Route 23 in Otis.

Strictly cross-country centers are at **Bucksteep Manor**, Washington Mount Road in Washington (413-623-5535), **Canterbury Farm**, Fred Snow Road in Becket (413-623-8765), both of which have rental shops; **Cranwell Resort**, at 55 Lee Road in Lenox (413-637-1364), has snowmaking capability if nature doesn't cooperate.

Kennedy Park in Lenox uses the driveways and bridle paths of an old hotel for skiing; begin at the Lenox House Restaurant on Route 7, north of the center of town. **Notchview Reservation**, on Route 9 in Windsor, has marked trails; access and a trail map will cost you less than a dollar, and you can use the warming hut and waxing center.

Energetic and experienced skiers can take on the trails of **Mount Greylock**, although on weekends the park's trails are heavily used by snowmobiles, which shatter the wilderness quiet most cross-country skiers seek. It's a 17-mile round trip to the summit, and you should check in at the Visitor Center on Rockwell Road, off Route 7 in Lanesborough.

The Williams Outing Club has a trail guide which describes all the local trails: you can get a copy and more information on trails from the Outing Club, Baxter Hall, Williams College, in Williamstown; 413-597-2317.

OUTDOOR ACTIVITIES

Snowshoeing, winter photography and wildlife tracking weekends are offered by the Appalachian Mountain Club at their Berkshire center at the **Field Farm**, 554 Sloan Road in Williamstown. **Snowshoes** are available for rent and lodging is provided in the farmhouse, a beautiful modern home owned by the Trustees of Reservations; 413-443-0011.

Pleasant Valley Wildlife Sanctuary, on West Mount Road off Route 7, which is an Audubon Society property, and **Kennedy Park**, also in Lenox, offer good trails for snowshoeing. **Hopkins Memorial Forest**, on Bulkley Street, off Route 7 in Williamstown, has several miles of trails that are good for snowshoes. **Main Street Sports and Leisure**, on Main Street in Lenox rents snowshoes.

Ice skating rinks can be found at the **Pittsfield Boys Club** on Melville Street, where public hours are Saturday and Sunday 2-3:45 p.m. (413-448-8258) and at the **North Adams Veterans Rink**, on South Church Street; 413-664-9474. You may be skating with a future Olympic star, since Nancy Kerrigan, Todd Eldridge and Paul Wylie all got their starts on Massachusetts public rinks.

Hancock Shaker Village, at Routes 41 and 20, west of Pittsfield, normally closed in the winter, reopens for Presidents' Week, with a full schedule of indoor and outdoor activities. Tours of the village and **sleigh rides** through its frozen meadows will be offered during the entire week, and special events are planned for both weekends. These usually include winter farm activities. This is one of the few places in New England where you can see old-fashioned **ice-cutting**. Before the days of electric refrigerators, ice was cut from ponds and stored in ice houses, where it was packed in sawdust and stayed frozen all summer; 413-443-0188.

A number of parks and reserves in the Berkshires have **snowmobile** trails. The largest of these are **Beartown State Forest** in Monterey, **Mount Greylock State**

Reservation, near Williamstown, **October Mountain State Forest** in Lee, **Pittsfield State Forest**, **Savoy Mountain State Forest** near North Adams, and **Tolland State Forest** in Otis. For information on state parks and reservations in the Berkshires, call 413-442-8928.

South Face Maple Farm, off Route 7 in tiny New Ashford, invites visitors to take a self-guided tour of their 4,000 tap sugaring operation every weekend during the season, usually mid- to late February into mid-March. In the sugarhouse, where you can watch the sap boiling, antique sugaring equipment is displayed. A full breakfast of French toast (made with home-baked bread) or donuts with maple cream are served all day; 413-628-3268. **Davenport Maple Farm and Restaurant** (413-625-2866) and **Gould's Sugar House** (413-625-6170), both in Shelburne, are restaurants with sugarhouses. At Davenport's, the boiling syrup is visible through a glass wall, so visitors can watch as they eat. You'll see signs for these on the main roads during their sugaring season, or you can call for directions, since some are on remote roads.

INDOOR ACTIVITIES

The Berkshire Museum, on 39 South Street in Pittsfield, is a wonderful community museum with exhibits in all fields of human discovery, but on a larger scale than most smaller museums. The collections of Hudson River School paintings, American primitives, silver and ancient art in their fine art galleries would be enough to put the museum on the art map of New England. But they also have a regional history section with early tools, Native American artifacts and early electrical equipment. In the natural sciences they feature an aquarium, more than 3,000 minerals and fossils, and several other collections worth seeing. Check their calendar for regular programs, lectures and musical events; 413-443-7171.

The Norman Rockwell Museum, on Route 183,

just outside the center of Stockbridge, has the largest collection of original works of the illustrator, who lived in Stockbridge. The museum often hosts special exhibits featuring other illustrators and their works; 413-298-4100.

The Sterling and Francine Clark Institute, 225 South Street, in Williamstown, is one of New England's premier fine art museums, with 33 paintings by Renoir in their permanent collections.

The Institute also has significant works by other French Impressionists, including the Degas sculpture "Little Dancer of Fourteen Years." Several of Winslow Homer's best-known paintings are here, with works of the European masters. Early American furnishings and silver, as well as Asian art round out the collections. In the winter they offer a film series. Admission is charged; 413-458-9545.

Also in Williamstown, the **Williams College Museum of Art** has a collection of over 10,000 works, which is especially strong in the ancient and modern arts. The museum has New England's finest collection of ancient Abyssinian sculpture. It is also noted for mounting extraordinary exhibits which then go on tour of art museums throughout the country; 413-597-2429.

West Country Winery, on Greenfield Road in Colrain, specializes in wines from locally-grown apples, blueberries and peaches, and in hard cider, all of which you can sample in their wine shop. Adjoining is a lunchroom with a farm market selling apples, jams, jellies and a few country crafts. The apple pie is great; 413-624-3481.

Hancock Shaker Village, open for the Presidents' Week school vacations, offers midweek and weekend indoor activities. These usually include baking classes, craft demonstrations and workshops, Shaker music and family meals. Shaker stoves demonstrate their efficiency as they warm the workshops and buildings; 413-443-0188.

A SPA RETREAT

Canyon Ranch in the Berkshires, 165 Kemble Street,

Lenox, is one of the country's finest resort spas, priced, of course, to match its mystique. And rightly so, since it offers a full medical staff and houses its spa facilities in a replica of the Petit Trianon. In addition to the herbal and aroma wraps, mud and salt treatments, massages, facials and other luxuries of a spa, you can take cooking or art classes and learn stress management. Indoor tennis courts and jogging track make it almost unnecessary to step outside at all; 413-637-4100 or 800-742-9000.

CHRISTMAS CELEBRATIONS

Early December: **Christmas at Hancock Shaker Village**: Sleigh rides, family craft workshops, musical performances and other activities fill a weekend. Admission is by donation of non-perishable food or a new toy; 413-443-0188.

December: **Christmas in Stockbridge**: The entire main street is redecorated to appear just as it does in the well-known Norman Rockwell painting. Vintage cars are parked as he depicted them.

December 26: Eight historic inns and homes in Lenox open their doors to the public for a **Holiday House Tour**. The tour is self-guided: after purchasing a ticket, you can drive to these turn-of-the-century homes and see them at your own pace; 413-637-3646.

EVENTS

December 31: **Brodie Mountain's Grand New Year's Eve Celebration** in New Ashford, features an elegant buffet and a wide variety of entertainment; 413-443-4752.

December 31: **First Night** festivities in Pittsfield ring in the New Year with a parade, musical performances, and fireworks; 413-443-6501.

Late January: Butternut Basin holds a **Kids' Festival**, with magic shows and storytelling, in addition to children's ski events; 413-528-2000.

Mid-March: Brodie Mountain's **Irish Olympics** brings plenty of non-skiing activities and a lot of silliness to the mountain, such as a downhill canoe race, slush-jumping contests, and cardboard box races, as well as Irish music and jig competitions; 413-443-4751.

Mid-March: Central Massachusetts has two major **St. Patrick's Day Parades**, easily reached from the Berkshires. They are usually held on different days, so be sure to check for the exact dates. In Worcester, the festivities begin on Park Avenue at Mill Street and includes 25 floats and 20 marching bands; for information, call Leo Quinn at 508-753-7197. Closer to the Berkshires is the nation's second largest St. Patrick's Day parade in Holyoke, beginning at the K-Mart Plaza on Route 5; call 413-534-3376 for details.

Late March: The Chester Hill Association in Chester holds a **Maple Fest** in the center of town, beginning with a farmers breakfast featuring maple syrup. Horse-drawn wagons take visitors on a circuit of four local sugarhouses, where they will see oxen pulling sap-laden sleds, and watch the process of boiling syrup. Sled dog demonstrations with Alaskan huskies and other winter activities highlight the day; for information call Misty Mountain Farm, 413-354-6337.

WHERE TO CURL UP BY THE FIRE

The Orchards, on Route 2 in Williamstown, is unabashedly first class, from the arched fireplace and tapestry-upholstered sofas of its parlor (where a proper— and delicious—tea is served daily to guests) to the antiques and carefully chosen reproductions in its large, bright guest rooms. Choose a room overlooking the courtyard garden, designed to be an attractive centerpiece year-round, with shrubs that remain colorful even in the snow. Find a book and curl up in the quiet library with its stained glass windows, and let the snow fall where it may; 413-458-9611 or 800-225-1517. Or you can reserve through DestINNations at 800-333-4667.

Riverbend Farm, also close to the center of Williamstown, but on Route 7, was built before the Revolution. Restored to its colonial interior appearance (with all the modern amenities tucked in discreetly), the inn looks much as it did when Ethan Allen stayed here. Fine paneling lines the walls and beds are clad in homespun coverlets; 413-458-3121 or 800-418-2057.

Field Farm, at 554 Sloan Road in Williamstown, is a unique B&B that's the scene of occasional weekend nature programs. Rooms are large and modern; private and shared-lodging rooms are available. Two of the guest rooms have working fireplaces. The building has access for wheelchairs. The setting is superb, on nearly 300 acres of protected land in the valley; 413-443-0011.

Old Inn on the Green and Gedney Farm, on the Village Green in New Marlborough, are twin inns on the same property: one was originally a stagecoach inn and general store, and the other served a Percheron barn. The latter's soaring ceilings and heavy rafters create an atmosphere for the simpler, but often dramatic furniture and decor. The inn is appropriately furnished in antiques and oriental rugs. Some rooms have fireplaces; 413-229-3131.

The Inn at Laurel Lake, on Route 20 in Lee, is almost equidistant (20-30 minutes) from Jiminy Peak and Butternut Basin ski areas, and you should ask about passes when you reserve. After a day in the snow, warm up next to their corn-burning stove or the fireplace in their parlor and enjoy a gracious afternoon tea. The inn also features a sauna and a music room with CDs and a collection of more than 1000 classical records; 413-243-1436.

The Country Inn at Jiminy Peak on Corey Road in Hancock, is a newly-built condo-style development, with suites and efficiencies and fully equipped kitchens. In the winter the inn provides daylong activities for children. A game room, steam room, whirlpool, and a cozy lounge with a fieldstone fireplace add the finishing touches; 413-738-5500 or 800-882-8859.

Red Lion Inn is such a landmark on Main Street that all directions in Stockbridge begin "From the Red Lion, go..." While you're not likely to spend much time in its porch rockers, except in late March, its wide porch gives you an idea of the comfortable atmosphere inside. Fine antiques and canopied beds in period rooms, more modest furnishings in some of the shared-bath quarters in the main building; 413-298-5130.

DINING

John Andrew's Restaurant, on Route 23 in South Egremont, serves Mediterranean food in the country setting of an old farmhouse. Filet of salmon is served with ricotta dumplings, roast pork with leeks. Wines are moderately priced; 413-528-3469.

Firelight adds a warm glow to the dining room at **The Old Inn on the Green**, in New Marlborough, quite likely the most romantic setting in the area. It's a scene straight from the 1700s with tapers burning in wrought-iron chandeliers. Saturday night is a fixed menu, and you'll need early reservations, since the menu is mailed in advance to regulars. Thursday, Friday, and Sunday evenings are a la carte; 413-229-3131.

Church Street Cafe, 65 Church Street, Lenox, serves healthy, creative food in a bright tidy environment. Influences are from all cuisines: you'll find couscous, Japanese dishes, and the general eclecticism of a New American menu; 413-637-2745.

La Bruschetta Ristorante, 1 Harris Street, is tucked away in a corner of West Stockbridge, serving creative dishes—roast pork is coated in toasted fennel, a raspberry tart is made with goat cheese—but it's not just clever for the effect. The bottom line is always the flavor, which will be fresh and interesting. Ask for directions when you reserve; 413-232-7141.

Hobson's Choice, 159 Water Street, Williamstown, is casual and inviting, with a substantial menu and good beer list. No real surprises on the menu, but a wide variety which includes several vegetarian entrees and a salad bar with every meal. They serve dinners only, from 5-9 daily, and reservations are recommended; 413-458-9101.

VERMONT:
THE GREEN MOUNTAINS

The stereotypical Christmas card view of Vermont—a snow-covered clapboard village clustered about its white church in the hollow of a mountain-ringed valley—is not the figment of an artist's imagination. Vermont, or at least much of it, does look like that. But to pass the state off as nothing more would be a mistake. Vermont has a far wider range of attractions than just its bucolic scenery, and most of them are within easy reach of its winter sports centers.

The Green Mountains form a 30-mile-wide barrier down the center of the state's 160-mile length. Their average altitude is 1000 feet, but several run over 3000 feet. Mount Mansfield, site of Stowe's ski area, is over 4000 feet. The Green Mountains are the oldest mountain range in New England, which accounts for their rounded summits. But don't let these gentle-looking giants fool you, however: they look a lot steeper from the top, and provide some very challenging terrain.

Because the mountains lie the length of the state, its ski areas are spread over a larger geography than those of the other New England states, with the southernmost only a few miles from the Massachusetts border and the northernmost almost on the Quebec line. As a result, much of the state is within the 30-mile radius of the ski areas that we have chosen to cover in this book.

To obtain a copy of the *Vermont Traveler's Guidebook*, as well as a state highway map and answers to specific questions, contact the Vermont Department of Travel and Tourism, 134 State Street, Montpelier, VT 05602; 802-828-3236. For winter travel information on Vermont, write or call for a copy of *Vermont Winter Guide*, a full color magazine-format publication with general information and a listing of lodgings throughout the state. Write to the Vermont Chamber of Commerce, P.O. Box 37,

Montpelier, VT 05601-0037 or call 802-223-3443. For information on the facilities at each ski area, contact the Vermont Ski Areas Association at 802-223-2439. The Vermont Association of Snow Travelers (VAST), which maintains and grooms snowmobile trails throughout the state, can be reached at 802-229-0005.

MOUNT SNOW/HAYSTACK

Not far from Vermont's southern border, the Mount Snow area has grown remarkably in the past decade, largely because of the ski area. Once a lazy little town, Wilmington is now a busy crossroads, and Route 100 through West Dover is lined by ski lodges and recreation-related businesses. The nearest cities are Brattleboro to the east and Bennington to the west, both on Route 9. The region adjoins the southern tracts of the Green Mountain National Forest

For more information on the area contact the Mount Snow/Haystack Regional Chamber of Commerce, P.O. Box 3, Page House, Main Street, Wilmington, VT 05363; 802-464-8092.

FOR THOSE WHO SKI

Mount Snow, which includes the 44 trails of the formerly separate Haystack Mountain, is the most southern ski area in Vermont, and the southernmost "big" area in New England.

This means it is sometimes crowded, but new lifts help keep lines down and 130 trails and 137 acres of tree terrain disperse skiers quickly. 60% of the trails are for intermediate skiers, and they have a strong emphasis on their ski school and facilities for learning skiers. Un Blanco Gulch, the first snowboard park in the east, continues to expand. 802-464-3333 or 800-245-SNOW.

Cross-country skiers will find fifteen miles of trails maintained by the Brattleboro Outing Club (802-254-4081) and nearly thirty miles at The Hermitage in Wilmington; 802-464-35111. **Timber Creek Cross Country Ski Center** is directly opposite Mount Snow; 802-464-0999. The Green Mountain National Forest offers almost limitless backcountry skiing.

OUTDOOR ACTIVITIES

Sleigh rides through the crystal evening air are available at **The Adams Farm**, where three double traverse sleds are pulled by Belgian draft horses. Or opt for a romantic 45-minute sleigh ride for two. Group rides that go for 90 minutes include a stop at a cabin deep in the woods, warmed by woodstoves, where guests enjoy hot cocoa and music from an old player piano. If you're there with kids, take them to the petting farm, where they can meet sheep, chickens and other livestock in person; 802-464-3762.

At **Fair Winds Farm** in Brattleboro, a two-horse team pulls a hay-filled sleigh through the woods, over the meadows and along the streams of their family farm. Daytime and evening rides are available by prior reservation; you can warm up in their wood-heated greenhouse or gather around an outside campfire if the weather permits. The farm operates largely on horse-power—the *real* kind—and produces organic vegetables in the summer. If you have a condo and are cooking your own breakfasts, you'll want to take home some of their fresh eggs, too; 802-254-9067.

Winter Walks are **snowshoe** treks in the Green Mountain National Forest, led by naturalist Lynn Levine, who points out and discusses tracks, trees, and other signs of nature in the woods; 802-464-3333.

Owl Moon Walks are guided hikes in the winter woods to observe owls and learn about them and their habitat. These take place each month during the full moon and are led by a naturalist; 802-464-3333.

Snowmobile tours of varying lengths, covering a 200-acre working dairy farm on Woffenden Road in Wilmington are given Monday through Saturday at the **Wheeler Farm**. You can stock up on **maple syrup** while you're here, too. Snowmobiles are provided; 802-464-5225. **Outpost Snowmobile Rental and Tours** provides what their name promises, with day or night trips on trails in the nearby National Forest. They also have packages that include lodging and meals; 802-464-5112 or

800-451-4289. **High Country Snowmobile Tours**, on Route 9, offers guided trips ranging from an hour to overnight; 802-464-2108 or 800-627-7533.

Snowmotion Snowmobile Tours operates day and night tours by reservation from Wilmington; 802-464-7750. **Rock Maple**, on Route 9 east of Wilmington, also has snowmobile tours; 802-464-3284 or 800-479-3284.

Twin Brooks Tours, west of Wilmington on Route 9 in Woodford, has tours on a wide range of backwoods trails through the Green Mountain National Forest, not only in the immediate area, but as far north as the Canadian border; 802-442-4054.

The **Ski Baba Trail**, near the Carinthia Base area at Mount Snow, is lighted evenings until 9 p.m. for sledding. Bring your own sled; 802-464-3333.

Bird hunting is offered throughout the winter at **The Hermitage** in Wilmington, a game farm that raises pheasants. Bring your own dog or use theirs; rental guns are available, as are hunting permits. Hunts are available in the morning or afternoon following the first snowfall, but by reservation only; 802-464-3511.

Memorial Park Skating Rink in Brattleboro, east on Route 9, rents skates; 802-257-2311. There is also a rink at the Carinthia Base Lodge at Mount Snow (802-464-3333) and at Beaver Brook Park in Wilmington; 802-464-8092.

In March and April, **Sprague's Sugarhouse** in Jacksonville makes maple syrup. You can watch the old fashioned wood-fired evaporator boiling the sap, see the display of antique equipment and enjoy the traditional New England sugar-on-snow (it's served with dill pickles to balance the sweetness) at their sugarhouse on Saturdays and Sundays; 802-368-2776.

INDOOR ACTIVITIES

Teens over age 15 have a dance club of their own at Mount Snow on Saturday evenings from 8 p.m. until midnight.

Planet 9 After Dark is reserved for that age group, with appropriate music and activities. Younger teens and children over ten years old have **The Cave Club** in the main base lodge with dancing, games and refreshments on Saturday evenings from 7 until 10 p.m.

North River Winery, south of Route 9 in Jacksonville, is open Friday through Sunday in the winter, offering free tours and tastings. It is accessible to wheelchairs; 802-368-7557.

At the top of Hogback Mountain, on Route 9 in Marlboro, the **Living History Museum** is open Saturday and Sunday in the winter from 10-5. Its exhibits cover five centuries, with a heavy emphasis on military history. This is not surprising, since the Association which created the museum is made up of reenactors who travel to battleground and other historic sites to stage historically accurate events. Since the museum is newly opened, its collections are still growing. Admission is by donation; 802-464-5569.

Just east of the Living History Museum, on the ground level of a shop carrying fine Vermont-made foods, is the **Southern Vermont Museum of Natural History**, with mounted specimens of birds and small animals native to the area; 802-464-5494.

Windham Brewery, on Flat Street in Brattleboro, gives tours on Saturday afternoons, with tastings of its seasonal beers. They have a restaurant too; 802-254-4747.

CHRISTMAS CELEBRATIONS

Early December: Brattleboro, east of Wilmington on Route 9, celebrates **Holly Days**, with carolers, roasted chestnuts, hot cider and other seasonal activities at various places in town; 802-254-4565.

Early December: Radio station WVAY sponsors a **Holiday Concert** at Memorial Hall in Wilmington. Admission is a donation to the local food shelf; 802-464-1111.

For the entire month of December everyone in the Wilmington/Mount Snow area joins in **The Nights Before Christmas**, with lighting displays, a living creche, torchlight parades, carol singing, fireworks, wreath-making workshops, displays of gingerbread, hayrides for the children, and a general festive air to all the shops, inns and lodges; 802-464-8092.

EVENTS

Late December: Mount Snow/Haystack holds a **torchlight parade and fireworks** display one evening between Christmas and New Years; 802-464-3333.

December: **Snocross World Series** brings snowmobile lap races at Haystack; 802-464-3333.

December 31: **Last Night Brattleboro** is a celebration of the season, with sleigh rides, sliding, skating, skiing, music, and entertainment throughout the town; 802-254-5054.

January 1: The Annual **Harriman Ice Fishing Derby** on Harriman Reservoir offers a first prize of $10,000; 802-368-7606.

Mid-February: **Torchlight parade and fireworks** at the ski area; 802-464-3333.

Late February: **Brattleboro Winter Carnival** is a week of family-oriented fun, with more than 50 different events. All the winter sports are represented, and there's a parade, sleigh rides, music, and sugar-on-snow. 802-254-4565.

Mid-March: A **Snowman Contest** at The White House Inn in Wilmington brings snow artists of all ages to compete for prizes; 802-464-2135.

Mid-March: **Vermont Products Day** is an annual event in West Dover, with maple syrup and candy, cheeses, jams and jellies, crafts and other specialty products made throughout the state on display and sale at the ski area; 802-464-3333.

Easter Morning: **Sunrise Service** at the summit of

Mount Snow begins the day, then skiers come down the mountain in search of eggs. One of these contains a free season pass for the following year; 802-464-3333.

SHOPPING AND CRAFTS

Wilmington, at the junction of Routes 9 and 100, seems to exist for the sole purpose of providing visitors a place to shop for crafts, food, antiques and other goods. Its main street, Route 9, is filled with shops and galleries.

At the Mountain Park Complex on Route 100, **Crafts Inn** sells specialty foods, handcrafts, woodenware, jewelry, hand-knit sweaters, and other products created in Vermont; 802-464-5337.

WHERE TO CURL UP BY THE FIRE

The White House is a landmark, high on its hill with the tracks of sleds radiating down its front lawn in the winter. Just as the hill was made for sliding, the inn was made for warming up. An indoor pool, whirlpool and sauna await after a day on their own cross country and snowshoe trails. They have a complete ski touring center; 802-464-2135 or 800-541-2136.

A former farmhouse that later became the summer estate of the *Social Register*'s editor, **The Hermitage** is now a country inn with 29 guest rooms spread among its several buildings. Individually decorated, many with fireplaces and all with antiques, rooms are comfortable and elegant. A collection of Delacroix prints and another of antique decoys decorate public areas. The innkeepers also raise pheasants, ducks, geese, wild turkey, and partridge as a hobby, and these are not only reflected in the inn's evening menu, but provide guests with the opportunity to hunt on the property. Guests can also watch the inn's maple sugaring operation late in the winter. the Hermitage is on Coldbrook Road in Wilmington; 802-464-3511.

Sno Goose Inn, in West Dover, has wood-burning fireplaces, Jacuzzi tubs, and a large Steinway Grand piano. Wine and hors d'oeuvres are served in the evening; 802-464-3984.

In a classic Cape Cod cottage beside Route 9 just west of Wilmington, **Nutmeg Inn** looks the perfect picture of a New England home. It's just as cozy on the inside, with wood-burning fireplaces, king and queen beds, and a full country breakfast every morning; 802-464-3351.

Shearer Hill Farm B&B is a small working farm on a country road, the picture of rural Vermont. Rooms are large and cross-country trails lead from the door; 802-464-3253 or 800-437-3104.

DINING

Skyline Restaurant wouldn't need to serve good food to keep a steady line at their door; people would come there just for the view. It sits atop Hogback Mountain, the state's only mountain with a major road running right over its summit. But the food is good, too. They are particularly known for their waffles and their omelets, but they serve lunch daily and dinner Wednesday through Sunday during the winter. They're on Route 9, east of Wilmington; 800-584-5156.

Le Petit Chef serves French food in a 200-year-old Wilmington farmhouse. Look for the classic dishes with an original flair; 802-464-8437.

Casual, with a youngish clientele, **Poncho's Wreck** in the middle of Wilmington, serves Tex Mex and other standards with few surprises, except for the escargot and the chicken curry; 802-464-9320.

STRATTON, BROMLEY AND THE MANCHESTER AREA

So adept is Manchester at the business and pleasure of hospitality that even confirmed winter-haters will have a good time here. It's one of those few places where you really can curl up for a weekend inside your inn and let the weather and the skiers do whatever they want to. The visual beauty of its setting, with Mount Equinox rising directly behind it, continues in the fine homes that line Route 7A, its main street, and the lanes along either side. These are not little cottages and farmhouses. They are nineteenth century homes built by the very wealthy who summered here. Most are still private homes, but remarkably few have become inns and B&Bs. It is to one of these that the winter traveler should repair and watch winter from a big comfortable chair beside the fireplace.

The Manchester Chamber of Commerce can provide events, schedules and other information on the area; 802-362-2100.

FOR THOSE WHO SKI

Family-friendly **Bromley** has an especially gentle "baby slope" for learners and small children, and sweeping views of Equinox from its south-facing trails. This southern exposure makes it warmer in the iciest part of the season and shelters it from some of the worst winds. A $19 midweek lift ticket and their new Flex Tickets make Bromley one of the best values as well. It is on Route 11, only a few miles east of Manchester Center; 802-824-5522, lodging 800-865-4786.

Glitzy **Stratton Mountain** is a self-contained world-class resort with slope-side condos, modern new base facilities, and its own village shops in Tyrolean architecture. Lifts, snowmaking and trails are all first class. On Route 30, about 10 miles south of Bromley; 802-297-2200, lodging 800-843-6867.

Magic Mountain, on Route 11 in Londonderry, has been reborn, after a few years out of operation, and it's better than ever. We like its casual atmosphere, and the fact that each trail gives skiers a little challenge. While still within the skill levels posted, a beginner trail will have a short stretch that borders on intermediate, while intermediate trails will stretch a skier's talents just a bit beyond, but only for a short distance. When you get to the point where you can whiz down a trail, you know you're ready to move up a notch. No glitz, but a nice lodge, short lines, low lift prices, lots of variety, and challenging trails for all levels; 802-824-5645.

Magic Mountain also has a **tubing park** with plenty of lanes and an all-terrain park for snowboarders.

The woods and meadows of **Robert Todd Lincoln's Hildene** are webbed with cross-country trails (802-362-1788), **Stratton Mountain** has a cross-country center (802-297-1880) and **Wild Wings Ski Touring Center** in Peru is a family-oriented cross-country facility (802-824-6793. For backcountry skiing on uncrowded and ungroomed trails, we like **Merck Forest**, a nature preserve in Rupert. This is what cross-country skiing was when we were kids: a chance to "hike" in the winter woods without someone breathing down your neck if you decide to stop and listen to the quiet of the woods. Trails and woods roads criss-cross the hillside terrain, providing plenty of options for beginners or experts. Donations are welcome; 802-394-7836. **Stratton Mountain** has more than ten miles of trails; 802-297-4063.

Outdoor Activities

Karl Pfister Sleigh Rides in Landgrove, near the Bromley ski area, has two 12-passenger traverse sleds with bench seats and one four-passenger sled. Day or evening rides last 45 minutes; 802-824-6320.

Sleigh rides and winter horseback riding are available at **Horses for Hire** in Peru. Rides in a two-horse sleigh pulled by Belgian horses include a campfire, hot cider and storytelling; 802-824-3750.

Stratton Mountain has one 10-passenger sled for 30-45-minute rides on weekends and holidays by reservation. Stratton also has a lighted outdoor **skating rink**, rentals and skating parties; 802-297-2200.

Vermont Institute of Natural Science, in co-operation with The Equinox Land Trust, offers programs in all areas of natural science, often in combination with other interests, such as art or photography. They operate a falconry school (where else can you learn this art?) and teach techniques of off-road ice driving and the gentle art of snowshoeing. Most of these take place on the extensive lands of Mount Equinox, which the hotel has put into a land trust to maintain its natural environment; 802-362-4374.

A wide variety of outdoor activities are on the busy schedule at **Merck Forest and Farmland** in Rupert, northwest of Manchester on Route 315. Their Winter Solstice Gathering, for example, features **sleigh rides** and other events include **snowshoeing, animal tracking, winter astronomy, and maple sugaring**; 802-394-7836.

The Dorset Historical Society provides a recorded **walking tour** of Dorset, which gives the history and architectural information on a number of the village's outstanding landmarks. One of these, the former Enfield Congregational Church chapel on the main street, was saved when the Quabbin Reservoir was built, flooding many old communities in that Massachusetts valley. Both the church and several other buildings in Dorset were taken down, brought north and reconstructed in the village. Not only is the tour interesting, but it is available on Saturday mornings year-round; you'll appreciate just how rare this is in small towns, where most town historical museums are usually open only in the summer. Pick up a tape recorder and book of photographs—thoughtfully provided to help you spot each building and landmark—at the Society's museum diagonally opposite the Dorset Inn; 802-867-4450.

Throughout the year, inns in Manchester and Dorset team up with the Vermont Land Trust and a group called **Conservation Inns** to present programs featuring protected lands, local farms and food products, and environmental education. Their purpose is to connect visitors to the region with the land around them, especially to the abundant conserved land and its possible uses. Programs center around special weekends, when guests at the participating inns have a wide choice of activities. Even the breakfast menus fit into the theme, featuring Vermont agricultural products, and chefs sometimes conduct cooking demonstrations, as well. These scheduled weekends may include an owl walk, a farm visit, an herb-cooking class, a wagon ride behind a team of Belgian horses, performances by a storyteller or musician, or a sugar-on-snow party. Participating inns in this area include **The Inn at Ormsby Hill, Barrows House, Cornucopia of Dorset, Equinox Hotel and Resort, Battenkill Inn**, and two Arlington properties, **Hill Farm Inn** and **West Mountain Inn**. Many of the activities are at **The Merck Forest and Farmland Center**; 802-375-2269.

INDOOR ACTIVITIES

Arlington Gallery, in the village of Arlington, south of Manchester on Historic Route 7A, is filled with the work of the town's long-time resident, Norman Rockwell. Many of the people who host at this unique museum are the actual models he used for the famous magazine covers displayed there. It's open from 10-4 daily, except in January, when it closes. Admission is free in the winter; 802-375-6423.

The Southern Vermont Art Center is housed in one of Manchester's many historic mansions, which was converted to gallery space for contemporary and other art. Shows change frequently. It's open Monday through Saturday for a small admission fee; 802-362-1405.

On Seminary Avenue in Manchester Village, the **American Museum of Fly Fishing** preserves the history and memorabilia of fishing, including fishing equipment that belonged to Daniel Webster and Dwight Eisenhower. Winter hours are weekdays only, from 10-4; 802-362-3300.

The Vermont Country Store, in the little valley village of Weston, could be listed under "shopping" but to us it's more of an indoor activity, saved for a blustery day when the warmth of its woodstove takes the sting off the weather and we can spend the afternoon browsing through its aisles. Along with the merchandise it sells are its antiques, including its original wooden display cases and the old high-button shoes hanging from the rafters. The store is the real thing, updated with good, reliable things you thought no one made anymore, like root beer candy and apple butter, dishcloths and popcorn poppers that don't plug into a wall. The building is original, too, with a rambling ell added since the days of our youth, when we used to take half an hour to spend a quarter on penny candy (and always ended up getting exactly the same thing we got last time); 802-362-2400.

A local site that has become a place of pilgrimage to thousands of recovering alcoholics, is **Wilson House**, on Village Street, once operated by "the Widow Wilson." Her grandson, Bill, was born here in 1895. Addicted to alcohol by 1935, Bill Wilson and Dr. Robert Smith of St. Johnsbury, Vermont, developed the 12-Step recovery process and founded Alcoholics Anonymous. Wilson House is again an inn, but one with a mission, rescued from near collapse in 1987, and owned by a foundation to restore and preserve it, not as a museum, but as a living memorial. It is not advertised as an inn, although its bright, cheery guestrooms are often filled. The house is staffed and maintained by volunteers; A.A. and Al-Anon groups meet there regularly. Across the green in front of the church is the house where Bill W. spent part of his childhood with his maternal grandparents; the house is open to visitors. Even in winter, the path to the graves of Bill W. and his wife, Lois, is a well-worn one. You can find them in the East Dorset Cemetery, south of the village on Route 7A, about 1.7 miles from the Wilson House. Bill's simple headstone is the eighth on the left from the tree stump toward the rear of the cemetery. Ask for a map at Wilson House; 802-362-5524.

The Dorset Historical Society, unlike most village museums that close for the winter, is open 10:00 a.m. until noon on Saturdays year-round, or by appointment during the week. Its collections include rare examples of Fenton pottery, which later gained fame as Bennington Pottery. Along with posters for long-ago pie suppers, you'll see farm implements, a collection of old photographs of the quarries, and the general assortment of quirky tidbits that make local museums so fascinating. They are nicely displayed and labeled, too; 802-867-4450.

CHRISTMAS CELEBRATIONS

On the first two Saturday afternoons in December, Manchester holds the annual **Christmas Tour of the Historic Inns**, with period music and dress, as well as short dramatic presentations.

Early December: Dorset lights its Christmas tree in the center of the village and everyone joins in a **Carol Sing**; 802-867-5747.

On the second weekend of December, the town of Arlington celebrates St. Lucia Day with a **Festival of Lights**. The town is decorated and filled with pageantry, as well as Swedish baked goodies. A craft fair and tree lighting are part of the festivities; 802-375-2800.

Mid-December: Some of Dorset's finest homes and inns hold an open house called **Prelude to the Holidays**, with seasonal decorations and refreshments; 802-867-4455.

Robert Todd Lincoln's Hildene is opened in the evenings between Christmas and New Years, for **candlelit**

tours. Lovely in any light, this country home of Abraham Lincoln's son is at its finest in the soft glow of flickering candles, decorated for the holidays. A horse-drawn sleigh (or wagon if there's no snow) takes visitors through the woods and up the long driveway toward the glowing mansion. Cookies and hot mulled cider are served; 802-362-1788.

The month of December takes on a festive glow throughout the Manchester area, beginning with the Regional Tree Lighting on December 1, the official kick-off for their annual **Prelude to Christmas.** Highlights include a pathway of 3,000 luminaries and Vermont's largest potluck supper. Yes, it's commercial because the area has a lot of businesses, but it's very people-oriented, too, and a lot of fun; call the Chamber of Commerce at 802-362-2100.

EVENTS

Late November: **Robert Todd Lincoln's Hildene** is open Thanksgiving weekend and decorated with dried flower arrangements by amateur and professional floral artists. Although the upstairs rooms are not open, the first-floor rooms are all on view; 802-362-1788

The **Manchester Music Festival** presents two holiday concerts, one in Manchester in late November and the other in Dorset in late December; 802-362-1956 or 800-639-5868.

Early December: **Community Celebration Day** in Weston brings the whole village out—and visitors in—for horse-drawn sleigh rides, wreath making, caroling, concerts and special events at local businesses; call the Weston Community Council at 802-824-5606.

The **Dorset Players** present their annual Christmas play the first two weekends of December, in their playhouse in the village of Dorset. Children under 12 are admitted free, and adult tickets are only $5. It is wise to get tickets for both in advance; 802-867-5570.

First Night at Stratton, on December 31, features a party and torchlight parade, ending with fireworks; 802-297-2200.

In late January, Stratton Mountain holds its annual black tie **Ski Ball**, with dining and dancing throughout the evening; 802-297-1886.

Early in February, Manchester holds its annual **Chili Challenge**, when the area's restaurants vie for the chili-champ title. You can sample all the entries at The Equinox Hotel, beginning at 5:30, voting for your favorite; 802-362-1439.

Early February: **Tubb's Snowshoe Festival** includes guided tours, volleyball and softball played on snowshoes, and instruction on the sport; 802-297-2200.

Late March: At **The Vermont Maple Syrup Experience**, several Manchester and Dorset inns team up with the Vermont Land Trust and the Merck Center for a weekend of maple-related activities. Menus feature maple dishes, and guests can choose from a full schedule that includes watching early sugaring methods and riding behind the team of Belgians as sap is gathered, visits and taste-tests at local modern sugarhouses, sugar-on-snow parties, animal tracking and winter tree identification hikes, snowshoeing, storytelling and a banjo concert; 802-394-7836 (Merck Center).

Easter: **The Weston Priory**, whose choir is as close to the divine as we shall know on this earth, begins Easter Sunday with a Vigil and Eucharist at 5 a.m., followed by a potluck breakfast A second Eucharist is at 11:30 a.m.; 802-824-5409.

SHOPPING AND CRAFTS

Manchester Center is a favorite of outlet shoppers, with several **outlet malls** featuring upscale brands: Mark Cross, Brooks Brothers, Burbury's, J. Crew, Coach, Cole-Haan, etc. After Christmas many of these have really good sales.

For a real factory outlet—as opposed to company-owned shops—visit **The Orvis Store**, headquarters of the oldest mail order store in America. Home furnishings, sturdy sportswear and country clothing and, of course, fishing equipment. Look in the basement for the best bargains; 802-362-3750.

Vermont State Craft Center has a shop opposite The Equinox in Manchester Center, that exhibits and sells the work of about 200 of the state's most talented designers and craftspeople. They also offer workshops and classes, which you can learn about by calling for a schedule; 802-362-3321.

At Stratton Mountain, the **Stratton Arts Festival Craft Shop** continues the fine tradition of the summer craft festival all year round; 802-362-0929.

Early December: The **Christmas Arcade** at the Manchester Elementary School is a fundraiser for local charities, featuring crafts and local shops; 802-362-4700 or 800-362-4747.

Long Ago and Far Away carries fine North American Indian and Eskimo art, along with a selection of work by Vermont artists and designers. Along with pottery and baskets, they have high-quality quillwork and other hard-to-find Indian arts. They are in the Green Mountain Village Shops near the intersection of Routes 30 and 11 in Manchester Center; 802-362-3435.

One of Vermont's best-known bookshops, the **Northshire Bookstore,** is at the intersection of Routes 30 and 7A in Manchester Center. It's a browser's paradise, with books on all subjects; 802-362-2200 or 800-437-3700.

Miniature doll collectors should go to **Enchanted Dollhouse** on Route 7A, two miles north of Manchester Center, where its twelve rooms are filled with toys, fine dolls, dollhouses and miniatures; 802-362-1327.

J.K. Adams Company, on Route 30 in Dorset, designs and manufactures fine quality woodenware, from bread boards and butcher blocks to wine racks. Their shop is at the factory; 802-362-2303.

A Spa Retreat

Manchester Village (not the commercial center with all the outlet shops, but the lovely old village just south of it) is dominated by the facade of **The Equinox**, a grand old hotel which has fallen on good times. Beautifully restored to its regal elegance—Mrs. Lincoln and the boys stayed there in its youth—it is now a full-service resort, with a health spa in its backyard. The staff there is helpful, friendly and not as unrelentingly bouncy as at many spas. They recognize that you are there for a vacation and a getaway as well as a healthy interlude, and good humor prevails. A large indoor pool is the centerpiece, surrounded by saunas, massage and herbal therapies, fitness equipment, and a gift shop. Their cross-country and snowshoe trails ascend the slopes of Mount Equinox, which rises directly behind the inn. Four-day spa packages include cross-country skiing or snowshoeing, a body composition analysis, an herbal wrap and other treatment of your choice, a daily massage, and exercise classes and personalized training; 802-362-4700 or 800-362-4747.

Where to Curl up by the Fire

Just south of Manchester Village on Route 7A, is the historic **Inn at Ormsby Hill**. The main house dates from 1764, and one of our favorite guest rooms, The Library, is found in this part of the house. History surrounds you: the home was once owned by Robert Todd Lincoln's law partner and President Taft was a frequent guest. In the previous century it had been a stop on the Underground Railroad. Each room is different, and each has a personality: impeccable and elegant, comfortable, but never cute or prissy. Most have windows that open over the double whirlpool tubs so you can watch the fireplace in the bedroom as you soak. Little details are thoughtful, like corkscrews, spare light bulbs, scissors, and a mending kit in each room. We could only find one thing to grumble at:

lighting in The Library made it difficult to read in bed, so we slept instead. Featherbeds mound on canopied beds so tall that guests need stepstools to climb into them. Innkeepers with a fine-tuned sense of humor set the tone for evening conversation as everyone gathers around the big fireplace in the comfortable den; 802-362-1163 or 800-670-2841.

Marble West Inn is another of our personal favorites, in a fine Greek Revival home typical of a style of construction popular in Dorset, where the first marble quarry in America opened before the Revolution. Even the grander homes in town were built of wood, on foundations of marble block, and decorated with marble porches, pillars or other embellishments. The inn, among the finest examples of this construction, was built in 1840 by George Holley, an important man in the marble industry for his daughter at her marriage to Spafford West, founder of the Norcross-West Marble Company. Its foundations, porches, steps, walkways, fireplaces and front columns are all made of marble. The interior is decorated with stenciling by the doyenne of modern stencilers, Adele Bishop; great names in the arts abound in Dorset, and you never know whose work—or who—you'll meet there. On weekend nights, don't pass up the chance to have dinner at the inn; they only serve inn guests, and only by prior reservation, but it's worth planning on. You'll get a sampling of their talents at breakfast, which is served in the elegant dining room. The owners are full of information on Dorset's colorful history. Rooms are beautifully furnished and enormously comfortable; 802-867-4155 or 800-453-7629.

Lodging is available at the **Trailside Condominiums** at Magic Mountain; 802-824-5620. Also within skiing distance of the lift line is **Dostal's**, an Austrian lodge with a long tradition of hospitality. Motel-style rooms are spotless and well furnished and the dining room serves wienerschnitzel and other international favorites. Package plans come with or without meals, but most skiers welcome the chance to settle in after a day in the snow, and opt for the good variety of menu choices here; 802-824-6700 or 800-255-5373.

One of the most unusual opportunities to curl up by a fire is deep in the woods of **Merck Forest**, where rustic cabins are available for rent during the winter. The only heat is a woodstove, and the only way to get there is on skis or on foot, but a weekend in one of these is an experience your family will always remember. In March, the center is busy with sugaring activity, a particularly interesting time to be living in their woods. You'll need to reserve in advance; 802-394-7836.

1811 House is in the center of Manchester Village, convenient to dining and shops, but quiet. Good taste glows from each room in this historic home, with guest rooms individually decorated in antiques and custom furniture. The quirky details of the old building have been preserved, but all the modern comforts have been discreetly added. Like much else in the village, the inn has a Lincoln connection; it was once the home of the President's granddaughter. The small pub downstairs specializes in single malt Scotch whiskeys. Fireplaces, fresh-baked cookies and congenial hosts add to its warmth; 802-362-1811 or 800-432-1811.

The Manchester View Motel combines some of the best qualities of a hotel and a motel. Rooms are spread among several buildings, each with mountain views. Half the rooms have fireplaces, many have whirlpool tubs and all are individually decorated. Rates are quite reasonable and family suites are a real bargain. During Manchester's "Prelude to Christmas" they offer three nights for the price of two. They are located north of Manchester Center on Route 7A, close to The Enchanted Dollhouse; 802-362-2739.

DINING

Our pick of local restaurants is the dining room at **Inn at West View Farm**, just south of the village of Dorset. The menu is filled with surprises, including game meats and lively combinations of ingredients, dishes such as

Rosemary Quail and Pan-seared Sesame Shrimp. Don't overlook the comfortable rooms of the inn itself as a place to stay; it was once a farmhouse that began taking in summer guests, and established Dorset as a summer retreat for artists and others who wanted to get away from city life and enjoy its relaxed atmosphere. You should make reservations for dinner here, even in slow seasons, since its consistent quality keeps the dining room busy; 802-867-5715.

For elegant, if expensive, dining, you can't beat **The Colonnade**, the formal dining room at **The Equinox** in Manchester Village. Its jacket-and-tie atmosphere is tonier than any other place in town, as is the menu. In the winter it's open only on Friday and Saturday evenings, and you'll need reservations; 802-362-4700

The Marsh Tavern, also at The Equinox, is less formal, with a cozy upscale pub atmosphere and a warming fireplace. Their salmon is so good we were tempted to order a second helping for dessert. They serve three meals a day and live music entertains patrons of the lounge on Friday and Saturday evenings; 802-362-4700.

Mulligan's, in Manchester, between the Center and the Village, is a bustling pub with hearty fare that runs from juicy big burgers to Maine lobster. The selection of ales is plentiful, the food dependable. Children's meals are an excellent value, starting at $1.50; 802-362-3663. Another branch is located at Stratton Mountain; 802-297-9293.

ASCUTNEY AND OKEMO

The Connecticut River forms the border between Vermont and New Hampshire, and its valley has provided an artery for travelers since the earliest settlers. Today, visitors enjoy both this history and the scenery. One of the few covered bridges over this river crosses between Windsor, Vermont, and Cornish, New Hampshire. The area was important in the origins of the precision tool industry, and the mansions of some of the early industrial magnates have found new life as inviting country inns.

The town of Chester is pure Victorian, with fine mansions clustered in its center, several of them offering lodging. For more information on the area, contact the Chamber of Commerce for the Mount Ascutney Region, P.O. Box 5, Windsor, VT 05089; 802-674-5910. The Chester Area Chamber of Commerce is at P.O. Box 623, Chester, VT 05143; 802-875-2939. For information on the Okemo area, contact the Ludlow Area Chamber of Commerce, P.O. Box 333, Ludlow, VT 05149; 802-228-5830.

FOR THOSE WHO SKI

Okemo is a modern, well-planned area with its heaviest emphasis on intermediate skiers. Slopeside condos are popular with families, who enjoy skiing out their backdoor. Glade skiing has been added recently. Okemo treads the narrow line between the glitzy resorts and the more intimate low-key places very successfully; nearly everyone enjoys its atmosphere. 802-228-4041.

Ascutney stands above the Connecticut River, one of the few of Vermont's ski areas that is not in the Green Mountain chain. Small and self-contained, it is known for its family orientation, real bargains for seniors, and easy access from I-91 and by train via Amtrak; 802-484-7711.

Cross-country enthusiasts will find 20 miles of groomed trails at **Tater Hill** in Chester (802-875-2517) and more than ten at **Fox Run** in Ludlow; 802-228-8871.

OUTDOOR ACTIVITIES

Native Sun Dogsledders, in Perkinsville, close to Ascutney, breed M'lot Malamutes, the largest strain of sled dogs. They reach 150 pounds in weight and are very fast, running in teams of seven or nine dogs. Trips lasting two to four hours include a campfire lunch; full-day trips are available for the really adventurous. Reserve well in advance for moonlight excursions, if you are lucky enough to be there when the moon is full; 800-699-SLED.

Taylor Farm, on Route 11 in West Londonderry, has **sleigh rides**, Friday through Sunday from noon until 8 p.m. For an extra $5 you can add a picnic by the fireside. You will need a reservation; 802-824-5690.

The Inn at Weathersfield offers daytime rides in their double-runner Town Express sleigh, which holds four or five passengers. Rides begin at the inn, by reservation only, and last about half an hour. The inn is on Route 106; 802-263-9217 or 800-477-4828.

In nearby North Springfield, **Hi-Lo Farm**, at 58 Reservoir Road, has 16- and 14-passenger sleighs, with hour-long rides by reservation; 802-886-8441.

Vermont Snowmobile Tours take beginners or experienced snow machine handlers on two-hour trail rides as soon as the snow covers the trails. They welcome children, too, who ride with the guides for greater safety. You should reserve ahead; 800-286-6360.

Okemo Snowmobile Tours, nine miles north of Ludlow on Route 100, offers instruction and guided tours for riders of all skill levels, from Tame Terrain to Radical Rides. Helmets and boots are included; 802-228-4041 or 800-328-8725.

Snow Country Snowmobile Tours, on Route 103 in Proctorsville (just east of Ludlow) has tours and rentals;

802-226-7529. Rentals and tours, including moonlight rides and trailside cookouts are available from **Stanley Bill's Sales, Service and Rentals** on Route 30 in Townshend; 802-365-7375.

For **ice skating** in Ludlow, go to Dorsey Park, where the rink is run by the Ludlow Recreation Department; 802-228-2849. In Springfield, near Ascutney Mountain, you can **ice skate** at The Commons; 802-885-2727.

Madrigal Inn, in Rockingham, sometimes offers a special package weekend in December that includes cutting your own **Christmas tree** at the nearby plantation of the Vermont Country Store; 800-854-2208 or 802-463-1339.

March brings maple sugaring, and several local sugarhouses welcome visitors. **Mitch's Maples** in Chester still uses 400 buckets along with tubing to gather sap, and has a wood-fired evaporator; 802-875-2348. In Ludlow, **Green Mountain Sugar House** has a gift shop and arranges sugaring parties by advance reservation; 802-228-7151.

In Springfield, **Valley Brook Farm** (802-885-2085) also uses buckets and **Woods Cider Mill and Sugarhouse** (802-263-5547) is a 200-year-old family farm. Both will arrange sugaring parties.

Indoor Activities

A ride on **The Green Mountain Flyer**, a scenic rail trip from Bellows Falls to Chester Depot, is even more scenic when the world is blanketed in snow. Although it doesn't run on a regular schedule in the winter, it makes special trips before Christmas and Valentine's Day and during maple sugaring season. On the Santa Express, Santa boards the train with his bag of goodies, and guests on the Valentine's Day ride get flowers, cider and doughnuts. During maple season, passengers can try sugar-on-snow at the Chester Depot. The ride is two hours long, and covers 26 miles of rail that passes a deep gorge and two covered bridges. The ride begins in Bellows Falls, about 15 miles south of Springfield on Route 5 (between exits 5 and 6 of I-91); 802-463-3069.

Green Mountain Sugar House in Ludlow offers a look at the modern methods most Vermont sugarbushes use today to extract syrup from maple trees. The syrup and candies are just as sweet as when the process was carried out with buckets and horse-drawn sleds, and you can buy these and other Vermont products in their shop; 802-228-7151 or 800-643-9338.

On Route 103 just south of Ludlow is **Joseph Cerniglia Winery**, where they make not only wines but also Woodchuck Draft Cider. Along with free tastings of dinner wines, dessert wines and cider, the winery offers a shop filled with wines, foods and Vermont-made gifts; 802-226-7575.

The American Precision Museum, in the center of Windsor, traces the history of the American precision tool industry and the idea that machines should have interchangeable parts instead of each piece fitting only the single machine it was made for. Miniature models of old mills and their machinery are as interesting as the huge room filled with actual machines from old mills and manufacturing plants. You don't have to be mechanically minded to enjoy this museum, but you should wear boots, since the floor is cold. In the winter the museum is open by appointment only, so call ahead to arrange a time; 802-674-5781.

Old Constitution House, on Windsor's main street, is the site of the signing of the constitution of the independent republic of Vermont, which preceded statehood. Collections include furniture from the 18th and 19th centuries. It's open Wednesday through Sunday, and the admission is free; 802-672-3773.

For other activities close to Ascutney, see *Woodstock*.

EVENTS

Early December: Chester's village green is lined with

decorated trees for the celebration of **Prelude to Christmas**, when the Clauses arrive to light the trees and villagers join a candlelight procession as they carol from church to church. Afterwards, everyone gathers for a caroling concert. Many people wear Victorian dress for the evening, which begins at 4 p.m.; 802-875-2444.

Early December: **Walker's Tree Farm** in Brownington, near Ascutney, stages a Christmas Fest with refreshments and sleigh rides. This is the time to choose and cut the perfect Vermont Christmas tree; 802-754-8487.

December: One evening between Christmas and New Year's Eve, Okemo stages a **torchlight parade and fireworks** display, with Okemo employees skiing down the mountain carrying lighted torches; 802-228-4041.

Late January: Ascutney's **Winter Carnival** includes events for non-skiers, such as hot air balloons and fireworks displays; 802-484-7711.

Mid-February: **President's Week Celebration** at Ascutney features family activities, ice skating, a torchlight parade, and beer and wine tastings; 802-484-7711.

February: **Sugar on Snow Celebration** at Okemo, when maple syrup becomes a sticky candy for all to sample, 802-228-4041.

Mid-March: Cavendish's **Sugar-on-Snow Supper** has been an annual event for forty years, so you'd better get there early. It is held at the Baptist Church, from 5:30-7 p.m.; 802-226-7885.

SHOPPING AND CRAFTS

A specially designed catwalk allows visitors to watch the entire process as glass blowers at **Simon Pearce's Glass Factory** in Windsor create delicate stemware, vases and bowls from molten glass. A full shop adjoins, where glassware is displayed with other fine crafts including weaving and woodenware; 802-674-6280.

You can't miss the grand facade of **Windsor House** in

downtown Windsor. Inside this historic building is **The Vermont State Craft Center**, filled with the work of more than 200 of the state's talented designers and artists. You'll find pottery, woodenware, glass, fabric arts, woolens, jewelry in all media, handmade paper, and fine foods. It is wheelchair accessible; 802-674-6729.

Chester's Victorian architecture is clustered around a tiny green, and its shops offer a good variety, with an accent on Vermont-made products. **Vermont Stoneworks** specializes in marble and other stone products, such as rolling pins, pantry boards; 802-875-4141. **Tea Pot Shop**, also on the green, carries teas and tea drinking accessories, including fine china pots; 802-875-4288. Between the two you'll find **Misty Valley Books**, where we've spent a few winter afternoons browsing. It's open Sunday afternoons, but closed on Mondays; 802-875-3400.

For books in Ludlow, go to **Chapter XIV** on Main Street, where books share space with cards and unique crafts, and places to sit while you browse; 802-228-GIFT.

Canvasworks, on Ascutney Notch Road in Perkinsville, sells painted canvas floorcloths, fireboards, placemats and decorative hangings. All the designs are in traditional and whimsical styles; 802-263-5410.

For more shopping options close to Ascutney, see *Woodstock.*

WHERE TO CURL UP BY THE FIRE

Hartness House Inn, in Springfield, is not just another gracious mansion-turned-inn. The interior has been carefully restored and furnished in tasteful antiques and reproductions appropriate to its turn-of-the-century era. A three-story open stairway rises from the foyer and public areas have lots of dark wood and upholstery. Fireplaces throughout the inn add to its general air of Victorian comfort. Our daughter described it as "having the air of an English country home, without the corpse." It has both a dining room and a tavern for relaxing. Every evening a volunteer guide takes guests to tour the historic observatory and see the antique telescope built by the original owner. Cabin Fever and Weekend Getaway packages make winter stays even more attractive; 802-885-2115.

You will recognize **Rowell's Inn**, on Route 11 in Simonsville (seven miles west of Chester) as a stagecoach hotel by its imposing architecture. Built in 1825, it is on the National Register. Guests in its five antique-filled rooms gather in the evening by the fire in the pub-like tavern room, then adjourn to a fine dinner in the intimate candlelit dining room. We especially like the two spacious bedrooms on the third floor, with their curved ceilings and grand carved beds; 802-875-3658 or 800-728-0842.

The owners designed and built **Madrigal Inn** themselves, following their vision of a retreat from the world and a center for the enjoyment of fine arts. They host frequent concerts in the double-storied foyer, which was specially designed for performances. A cross-country trail leads from the back door, and a ski room makes storage of equipment easy. Rooms are bright, spacious, and comfortable, with extraordinary soundproofing and safety features. Handicapped access not only meets highest standards, it sets a few new ones. A large library offers a good range of books and board games. The inn is at 61 Williams Road, off Route 103 in Rockingham; 802-463-1339 or 800-854-2208.

Inn Victoria, in the center of the Victorian village of Chester, is unabashedly romantic, in the best tradition of Victorian exuberance. Lace, antiques, and a warm atmosphere fill the elegant home. Afternoon tea is served (see *Dining*, below), as are light dinners, the latter by reservation only. If offered, don't miss the scrambled eggs at breakfast; 802-835-4288 or 800-732-4288.

Button Farm Lodge, less than four miles from the Ascutney ski area, is a cozy and very reasonably priced B&B. On the property are Christmas trees, a good sledding hill, snowmobile trails, a pond for skating, and trails for cross country skiing and snowshoeing; 802-484-3300.

Close to Okemo, in the village of Ludlow, **The Andrie**

Rose Inn is luxurious with whirlpool tubs in view of the fireplaces, double steam showers, antiques, fine linens and a general well-heeled air. Dinner is served by candlelight on Saturday evenings; 802-228-4846 or 800-223-4846.

Those who prefer the feel of a private home to the busier atmosphere of an inn will like **The Inn at High View.** Its setting high on a hill in Andover makes it a little tricky to find (they'll give you good directions when you reserve), but it's worth looking for, in order to sink into their deep couches or relax over a fine dinner. Rooms are well-decorated, with views from every window. You will feel at home the minute you arrive; 802-875-2724.

High on a hill overlooking Windsor is a beautifully preserved mansion of particular architectural interest. **Juniper Hill Inn** balances grandeur with warmth, largely due to the engaging and energetic innkeepers; this is not just a turn of phrase, it takes real energy to keep a place this large warm with a wood furnace. Once there, you don't have to travel down the hill to dinner on Friday or Saturday evenings since it's served by the fireplace in the elegant dining room, by reservation only. Guest rooms have fireplaces, too, along with canopy beds and large windows. Once here, you may not care that there's good snowshoeing, winter hiking and sleigh rides nearby; 802-674-5273 or 800-359-2541.

Ascutney Mountain Resort has nearly 300 condo units right at the base of the mountain, with a restaurant, complete fitness center, indoor pool and shops. It's very low key and not as glitzy as many other condo villages, but great for families who don't need the packaged entertainment of other resorts; 802-484-7711 or 800-243-0011.

DINING

On the first floor of **Inn Victoria** is a tearoom where guests and others enjoy exceptionally good scones, homemade preserves, and assorted teacakes with their properly brewed English tea. Lunches include the traditional plowman's plate. A shop featuring teas and tea-related things adds another reason for visiting this elegant village home; 802-835-4288 or 800-732-4288.

Leslie's, in Rockingham, a stone's throw from I-91 south of Ascutney, is almost fanatical about fresh ingredients: the restaurant harvests 250 tomato plants over a typical summer. It's difficult to classify the cuisine: the daily poultry special could be quail or the chef-owner's newest chicken breast creation. Fine crafted wooden furnishings create a stylish air, but the restaurant is very casual. Both parents and children will be comfortable here; they prepare chicken and pasta dishes specially designed for children; 802-463-4929.

Penelope's is a casual lunch spot in the center of Springfield, serving generous sandwiches, soups, and salads plus a long list of entrees including sauteed scallops with cheddar cheese sauce and veal sauteed in marsala with ham and mushrooms. The restaurant is actually half bar and half restaurant, and handles both clienteles easily; the place is very popular with families. The dinner menu is standard American pub fare, salads, burgers, and munchies; 802-885-9186.

Echo Lake Inn, near Okemo on Route 100 in Tyson, serves a varied selection of creative dishes, such as game sausages or trout with a delicately seasoned garnish of artichokes. The menu changes often, and nightly specials reflect the very freshest ingredients of each season. Dinner is served by candlelight in an intimate, warm atmosphere; 802-228-8602.

SUICIDE SIX AND WOODSTOCK

In 1934, when skiing was a sport for the hardy adventurer who climbed the mountain before skiing down it, a group of skiers in Woodstock rigged a rope tow on a hillside at Clinton Gilbert's farm and powered it by an old Model T engine. The sport was ruined, moaned the purists, and it did indeed change markedly. This first rope tow in America was the beginning of the modern ski industry and the birth of Vermont as a year-round vacation destination.

For many years, Woodstock was famous for its gala Winter Carnival, filled with sporting events for hardy outdoors enthusiasts. The winter carnivals are no more, but the annual Wassail celebration the second weekend in December is a community event that cheerfully makes room for the town's visitors as well. Trees and windows glow with lights and shops are decorated for the holidays. The weekend's highlight is the parade of horse-drawn carriages and wagons.

Speaking of horse-drawn carriages, it is important to remember that all vehicular traffic in the town should move very little faster than a horse-drawn vehicle's pace. The speed limit is very low, and enforced by a team of vigilantes who delight in catching out-of-state drivers going even one mile per hour over the limit. No warnings, just a hefty fine. If you think ski-lift tickets are expensive, try a "speeding" ticket in Woodstock.

For information on the region contact the Woodstock Area Chamber of Commerce, P.O. Box 486, Woodstock, VT 05091; 802-457-3555.

FOR THOSE WHO SKI

Suicide Six, with only a 600-foot vertical drop, is a mouse named Simba, so don't let its name intimidate you. But its 19 trails do offer challenges as well as gentle terrain for beginners. It shares with Stowe the distinction of being Vermont's oldest ski slope; 802-457-1666.

The **Woodstock Ski Touring Center**, at the Woodstock Country Club on Route 106 has more than 30 miles of trails and carriage roads in the park-like setting of Mount Tom and along Kedron Brook; 802-457-6674.

NATURAL ATTRACTION

A short distance east of Woodstock on Route 4 is the dramatic **Quechee Gorge** (pronounced KWEE-chee), over which the road passes on a high arched steel bridge. Parking is provided at either end, so you can look down from the sidewalk on either side of the bridge into the deep gorge. It's quite impressive.

OUTDOOR ACTIVITIES

A sleigh ride along the Ottauquechee River and across the snow-covered fields and pastures of **The Billings Farm** includes a warming cup of hot cider, although the woolen lap robes in the farm sleigh will keep you toasty during the ride. These are usually held during the Christmas season and two weekends, one in mid-January, one in mid-February, and by reservation; 802-457-2355 or 457-2221.

In South Woodstock, the **Kedron Valley Stables** offer two work sleds with benches, several sleighs that can hold from 5 to 14 passengers, and a three-seater hotel sleigh which you can reserve for rides of 45 minutes to an hour. They are open daily, with rides beginning on the hour from 10-4, weather permitting. The stables are right on Route 106, just north of the Kedron Valley Inn; 802-457-1480.

A **skating rink** is located at Vail Field on Route 106 just south of Woodstock Village. Woodstock Sports rents skates; 802-457-1568. In nearby White River Junction, **B.O.R. Rink** on Highland Avenue, offers **ice skating** with rentals; 802-295-3236 or 295-5036. In Fairlee, **Lake Morey Inn**, just off Route 5 at the exit to I-91, offers **outdoor skating** on its outdoor rink, lighted   every Saturday night. Rental skates ($5) are available here, too; 802-333-4311.

Visiting children are welcome to join local kids on their favorite **sledding** hill at the Mount Tom School in Woodstock, a mile north of town on Route 12.

More than 25 species of hawks, eagles and owls are permanent residents at the **Vermont Institute of Natural Sciences Raptor Center**, a nature preserve dedicated to rehabilitating injured birds of prey. Along with the birds of prey, the center has ungroomed trails perfect for snowshoeing. You can warm up in the Visitors Center, where live exhibits include snakes and wood turtles. Winter programs are varied and include nature walks aimed at learning to identify wildlife by their tracks. The center is on Church Hill Road in Woodstock, and open Monday through Saturday from 10-4, November through April; 802-457-2779.

Another nature center with snowshoe trails is located in nearby Norwich. **Montshire Museum** sits on 100 acres along the banks of the Connecticut River, and its trails are marked with interpretive signs that help you understand the natural history of this part of Vermont. During the winter the museum sponsors a number of outdoor events, including dog-sledding and igloo building (see *below*); The museum entrance is on Route 5, south of the village, reached from exit 13 of I-91; 802-649-2200.

Although it's not, strictly speaking, an outdoor activity, it would be a shame to spend time in Woodstock and miss one of its most unique features, its five **Paul Revere bells**. Two are displayed where they can be seen, the oldest on the porch of the Congregational Church, and another at the Woodstock Inn. The others are where they can be heard, in the Universalist Church, the Masonic Temple and Street James Episcopal Church. Woodstock is the only town in America with five Revere bells.

INDOOR ACTIVITIES

Billings Farm and Museum offers a look at Vermont in the last century, and at the timeless quality of farming. One of America's oldest working dairy farms, its workings are interpreted through lively tours, demonstrations and programs. The restored farm kitchen is always busy and the creamery shows how butter was made. Children especially enjoy visiting the sheep and Jersey cattle in the barns. A museum shop sells books about Vermont and farming, as well as period gifts and craft kits, an excellent source of Christmas gifts for children. Open weekends in December and every day (except Christmas) during the last ten days of December as the farm prepares for Christmas, it is also open for a number of weekend programs throughout the winter. See *Outdoor Activities* below for sleigh rides on the farm. Send or call for a schedule or pick one up after you arrive in Woodstock. The museum is on River Road, close to the village center; 802-457-2355.

Dana House, the Woodstock Museum and headquarters of the Historical Society, is open on weekends throughout the winter. Its rooms are furnished in fine antiques, many of which were made by local cabinetmakers. The museum is at 26 Elm Street in the village center; 802-457-1822.

The **Vermont Institute of Natural Science**, on Church Hill Road, holds indoor nature programs for children and adults, usually dealing with Vermont wildlife. These feature slides or movies, stories, and hands-on activities; 802-457-2779.

Sugarbush Farm begins its maple syrup production in late winter, but welcomes visitors to the sugarhouse all winter. Inside it is set up to show the entire process from collecting the sap to boiling it down. Their shop carries Vermont cheese and jams as well as maple products. Call first to find out the condition of their road, since sugaring season is locally known as mud season for a very good reason. From Route 4 at Taftsville, follow the signs from the covered bridge to Hillside Road; 802-457-1757.

Not far from Woodstock, in Norwich, the **Montshire Museum** (see location *above*) has two floors of hands-on exhibits designed to teach both adults and children about technology and the natural world. Giant aquariums display sea life and freshwater creatures. See *Outdoor Activities* below for snowshoe trails; 802-649-2200.

In White River Junction, **Catamount Brewing Company**, the first of Vermont's modern breweries (there was brewing aplenty done in the old days, but the last of them had been closed for more than a century when Catamount opened) gives tours and tastings of their distinctive ales and lagers; 802-296-2248.

Across the river in New Hampshire, Hanover offers the attractions and activities of Dartmouth College, including top name performances at the **Hopkins Center** (603-646-2422) and the permanent and special exhibits at the **Hood Museum of Art**. The latter is especially strong in Oceanic art and European prints, but its permanent collections also include American, Asian, African, Native American and modern art. Special exhibitions may cover any era or artist, and are often introduced with docent-led gallery tours at 2 p.m. on Saturdays. Admission is free; 603-646-2426.

In Randolph, almost directly north of Woodstock on Route 12, is the world's only manufacturer of large disk music boxes. Tours of the **Porter Music Box Museum**, are offered on week days (except holidays) until 5 p.m. before Christmas and until 4 p.m. through the rest of the winter. A small admission is charged. In the museum you can see and hear antique and rare music boxes and a reproducing piano, an instrument that mimics the music of the person playing it. The museum is wheelchair accessible; 802-728-9694 or 800-635-1938.

SHOPPING AND CRAFTS

The village of Quechee is off the main road, clustered around a dam and a covered bridge. In the old mill buildings are elegant shops and the studios of **Simon Pearce Glass.** The hydroelectric turbine operates in full view on the lower level, where you can also watch glass-blowers at work creating some of the glassware sold in the shop above, along with pottery, handmade furniture, and other fine handwork. The showroom is open daily 9 a.m. to 9 p.m. year round; 802-295-2711 or 800-774-5277.

On Route 4, near Quechee Gorge, is a group craft shop called **Quechee Gorge Village**, although locals still call it by its former name of Timber Village; 800-438-5565.

The entire village of Woodstock is lined with boutiques and high-taste shops featuring art, antiques, clothing and other temptations.

CHRISTMAS CELEBRATIONS

Early December: Hanover, New Hampshire, begins its seasonal celebrations with **A Dickens of a Christmas**, an evening of caroling, music, street performances, a visit from Santa and the lighting of the town's Christmas tree; 603-643-3115 or 603-643-3512 at Hanover's information booth.

Second weekend in December: **Woodstock Wassail Celebration** fills the town with all the nostalgia of an old-fashioned Christmas, with caroling, a carriage and wagon parade, a handbell concert, a "Messiah" sing, trees and windows lighted and shops decorated for the holidays. Bring an offering for the Goodwill Wagon, which is filled by townspeople and visitors with gifts of clothing and food for families who would not have a Christmas without it; 802-457-3555 for Wassail Weekend schedules. For parade information, call the Green Mountain Horse Association at 802-457-1509.

The Norman Williams Public Library has its **annual booksale** during Wassail, with Santa arriving by horse-drawn wagon; 802-457-2295.

Early December: Ludlow has a **Community Christmas Carol** at Black River Academy, with refreshments following the carol sing.

Late December: Woodstock Inn & Resort holds an annual **Gingerbread House Contest** with inn guests as judges. The houses are displayed at the inn through New Year's Eve; 802-457-6614.

EVENTS

Thanksgiving Weekend: A holiday **Food and Craft Show** is held at the Woodstock Inn; 802-457-1100.

Mid-December: **Night Fires**, in White River Junction, is an arts performance inspired by ancient winter solstice celebrations. Storytelling combines with music, song, dance, poetry and drama into a program suitable for all ages; 802-863-1024.

Mid-January: **Dog Sled Day** at the Montshire Museum features an entire Saturday of dogsled demonstrations by mushers and their husky teams. Some of the visitors will be lucky enough to hitch a ride as the teams strut their stuff around the museum's riverside property, but everyone will have a chance to meet the malamutes and huskies and get a close-up look at a dogsled. Indoor exhibits in the museum relate to sled dogs, as well; 802-649-2200.

Late January: **The Brookfield Ice Harvest**, at the Floating Bridge on Sunset Pond in Brookfield, just off I-89 north of Woodstock, is a rare opportunity to see and participate in the collecting of ice as New Englanders did every winter before the refrigerator became standard kitchen equipment. Using historic tools and methods, everyone—visitors included—pitches in to cut, haul and store blocks of ice that can last all summer. The occasion is enhanced by sleigh rides, an ice sculpture demonstration and other winter activities; 802-276-3959.

February: **Dartmouth Winter Carnival**, in Hanover is a spectator event for its snow sculptures. Giant figures grow in the snow-covered lawns of the fraternity houses, and it's as much fun to watch them in the building process as to see the finished works of art; 603-795-2143.

Late February: **The Great Igloo Build** at the Montshire Museum gives everyone a chance to learn this ancient Arctic skill. Participants begin by learning to cut snow blocks, then to carry and stack them. By the end of the day a small village of igloos has sprung up. One of them could be yours; 802-649-2200.

WHERE TO CURL UP BY THE FIRE

If you are driving north to Woodstock on Route 106, you pass through the village of South Woodstock, and see the **Kedron Valley Inn** directly ahead of you as the road makes an elbow turn. It's a lovely sight at any time of day, any time of year, but just at dusk on a winter evening, it's enough to take your breath away. The inn is just as nice inside, with individually decorated rooms that are classy, but always comfortable. Most guest rooms have original hooked rugs designed by Claire Murray and all rooms have quilts.

Other examples from the owner's collection of quilts and vintage needlework decorate the walls. Guest rooms are in three buildings, two of them historic landmarks as stops on the Underground Railroad; our favorite room to curl up in was once one of the hiding places, its stairs cleverly hidden in a closet. It's a seven-minute drive to Woodstock, but we suggest reserving a table for dinner in the inn's excellent restaurant (see *below*); 802-457-1473 or 800-836-1193.

The Lincoln Inn at the Covered Bridge is a Victorian farmhouse with six homey, comfortable guest rooms and a dining room which serves the innovative—and inspired—continental specialties of its Swiss chef/owner. It's three miles from the center of Woodstock, at the Lincoln covered bridge; 802-457-3312.

Woodstock Inn and Resort is unusual for a full-service resort, because it sits directly in the center of town. Whatever happens in Woodstock, you have a front-row seat. Luxury rooms, a sports center, tavern, cafe, dining room, shops in the lobby, all the services you expect in a resort are here, along with the convenience of Woodstock outside the door. The Sports Center offers indoor tennis, squash and racquetball courts, a lap pool, whirlpool, Nautilus, aerobics, steam bath, saunas, and massage room. Their cross-country touring center rents snowshoes, but inn guests can opt for packages that include rental and use of more than 30 miles of trails. It's not intimate, with almost 150 rooms, but it's luxurious enough to make up for it. During Woodstock's Wassail Celebration the inn offers a special package that includes lodging, a buffet dinner, admission to the Cotillion Dance, and a holiday decorating workshop; 802-457-1100 or 800-448-7900.

North of Woodstock, in Brookfield, where the annual ice harvest takes place each January, **Birch Meadow B&B** has luxury log cabins, with woodburning stoves, lofts, and fully equipped kitchens. Privacy, on more than 200 acres of panoramic views, with cross country and snowshoe trails, tobogganing and hay rides; 802-276-3156.

Don't overlook the possibility of staying across the river in Hanover, a lively town with god restaurants. **The Hanover Inn**, opposite Dartmouth College (which owns it) is gracious and timeless, but with every modern service and amenity. Rooms are stunning and the hospitality is warm. It is perfect for you to attend events at the Hopkins Center next door, since the two buildings are connected by a tunnel. You don't have to wear boots to get home from the theater, even on a snowy night; 800-443-7024.

DINING

At the **Kedron Valley Inn**, every dish gets infinite attention from a highly skilled chef. Don't skip the appetizers; share one if you must, but be prepared to fight over the last morsel. Lamb is roasted to perfection and somehow the chef manages to cook salmon to just the right point while it is hiding inside a delicate puff pastry. Nice combinations, such as chicken with pistachios add life to the menu. We suggest ordering the "tasting menu," which allows you to sample a variety of the chef's latest creations. Be sure to reserve, since this place is no secret; 802-457-1473.

In the center of Woodstock, **Bentley's** is lively and spirited, with an interesting menu. Pan-seared trout, lamb medallions with black plum glaze, steak flamed in Jack Daniels, or an appetizer salad of sliced lamb, pecans, apples and tomatoes are some of the dishes we've enjoyed there. Lunches are far from ho-hum, too; 802-457-3232.

The Lincoln Inn at the Covered Bridge is one of our favorite dining rooms in Vermont. Dinner is always delicious and filled with delightful little surprises. Flavor combinations are imaginative and always work; presentations are beautiful and include the chef's signature carved vegetables. Our seafood dish was surmounted by a tiny carrot goldfish, and a mallard floated atop an entree of duck. Be sure to make reservations even in the winter, since we are not the only ones who will travel miles to eat here. It is three miles from the center of Woodstock on Route 4, at the Lincoln covered bridge, and dinner is served Tuesday through Sunday from 6-9 p.m.; 802-457-3312.

The Daniel Webster Room, in The Hanover Inn in Hanover, New Hampshire, is an outstanding restaurant in an elegant setting. The menu combines influences and inspirations from the best cuisines throughout the world, offering a cosmopolitan and sophisticated menu. It is worth traveling a bit to have dinner here; 603-643-4300.

A Hanover favorite, with the feel and warmth of a neighborhood pub, is **Patrick Henry's.** Sandwiches are a cut above the ordinary, and entrees are generous and hearty, such as beef stew or pesto lasagna; 603-643-2345.

Also in Hanover, **Café Buon Gustaio** serves northern Italian dishes in a casual/chic atmosphere; 603-643-5711.

KILLINGTON

U nlike most of the ski areas that developed near existing towns, Killington was carved out of a long and largely undeveloped valley. Its long access road created plenty of space for the lodgings, restaurants, entertainments and services required by such a large ski resort, and only a little of this has spread out onto Route 100. Those who like an active nightlife will find it here. The après ski scene is rated tops in New England, and the atmosphere is more like its Rocky Mountain counterparts.

To learn more, contact Killington and Pico Areas Association, P.O. Box 114C, Killington, VT 05751; 802-773-4181.

FOR THOSE WHO SKI

Killington is the biggest ski resort in New England, with six mountains of interconnected trails and lifts that now incorporate the former Pico Peak area. A new, more self-contained area is designed especially for families. Although it is strongest in easy trails (36%), the sheer number of trails (212) means that it has more of every kind of skiing than anyone else. Killington is just east of Rutland, off Routes 100 and 4; 802-422-3333. For recorded ski conditions call 802-422-3261; for lodgings 800-621-MTNS.

Cross-country skiers will find more than 35 miles of trail at **Mountain Top Ski Area** in Chittenden; 802-483-6089.

OUTDOOR ACTIVITIES

A good way to learn how to drive a snowmobile is to sign on for a tour with a guide who not only knows the trails, but knows the equipment and can show you how to use it safely. **Killington Snowmobile Tours**, on Killington Road, has tours for all skill levels, and along with providing instruction, they provide helmets and boots. You'll need a reservation; 802-422-2121. In Pittsfield, a little north of Killington on Route 100, **Outerlimits Snowmobile** Tours, at the Clear River Inn, also operates tours; 802-746-8611. At the **Cortina Inn** they rent snowmobiles for independent use, although they do have trails on the property where you can ride; 802-773-3333.

Cortina Inn is also the place to go for sleigh rides. 20-minute rides in a sleigh pulled by a team of Belgian horses; they leave regularly between 6 and 9 p.m., but you should still make a reservation; 802-773-3333. **Mountain Top Inn and Resort**, on Mountain Top Road in Chittenden, gives 45-minute rides in their two 12-passenger Austrian sleighs, by reservation; 802-483-2311 or 800-445-2100.

The **Pittsfield Inn**'s large antique sleigh is drawn across the meadows by a pair of Belgian horses. Rides are offered daily, by reservation; 802-746-8943. **Escape Routes**, headquartered at the inn, offers outdoor adventures, including **snowshoeing**; 802-746-8943.

The nearest ice skating rinks are in Rutland, a short trip via Route 4. **Giorgetti Ice Skating Rink** (802-775-7976) and **Royce Mandigo Arena** both offer public skating. The latter rents skates and offers lesson, too; 802-773-9416.

Outdoor rinks and ponds are fairly plentiful—try the rink at the **Cortina Inn**, where they also rent skates. **Mountain Top Inn**, in Chittenden, has an outdoor skating rink with rentals available; 802-483-2311 or 800-445-2100. **Summit Pond** also has skating; 802-422-4476.

Indoor Activities

President Calvin Coolidge State Historic Site has special winter exhibits in the Aldrich House, once home of the President's stepmother. These provide information about Coolidge's career and the village where he grew up. A brochure outlines a walking tour of the village, or you are welcome to snowshoe on the newly-built trails through the fields and forest. Plymouth Notch is on Route 100A, between Woodstock and Route 100; 802-672-3650.

Plymouth Cheese Corporation, once owned by the Coolidge family, welcomes visitors to its factory to see how Vermont cheddar is made, and sample some. The shop sells other Vermont-made goodies as well; 802-672-3650.

EVENTS

Thanksgiving Weekend: A juried **craft show** is held annually at the Cortina Inn at Killington; 802-422-3783.

Mid-December: **Night Fires**, in Rutland, is a multi-arts presentation based on ancient midwinter solstice celebrations. Its script weaves storytelling with music, song, dance, poetry and drama into a program suitable for all ages; 802-863-1024.

Late January: Killington's **Winter Carnival** includes snowshoe events, dogsleds, snow sculptures a chili cook-off, and plenty of après ski revelry; 802-422-3333.

WHERE TO CURL UP BY THE FIRE

Mountain Top Inn, in Chittenden (north of Route 4 between Killington and Rutland) is a self-contained resort with a cross-country ski center on 1300 acres of hilltop. Its country inn atmosphere, stunning views and fine dining make it as attractive to those who never intend to step outside as it is to those who enjoy its skiing, skating, sledding and sleigh rides; 802-483-2311 or 800-445-2100.

Restored to its 1835 charm, **Pittsfield Inn**, on Route 100 north of Killington, offers a full range of winter sports in addition to comfortable lodging and a good restaurant; 802-746-8943.

Killington Reservation Center offers one-stop shopping for all their condos and chalets, many of which are slope-side; 802-422-3244 or 800-338-3735.

The Inn of the Six Mountains combines modern architecture and amenities with the traditional feel of a classic ski lodge. It has full resort facilities to enjoy while everyone else skis: large pool, fitness center, massage therapist, indoor and outdoor hot tubs, sauna and a fireside lounge. Rooms are large and furnished in the trim clean lines of a European lodge; 802-422-4302 or 800-228-4676.

Tulip Tree Inn is Killington's smallest, with only eight rooms, but most have Jacuzzis, and the dining room is right downstairs, so you don't have to put your boots on to go to dinner; 802-483-6213 or 800-707-0017.

The Vermont Inn is a classic country inn, with some newer luxuries added: hot tub and sauna top the list. Their restaurant is well known for its fine fireside dining; 802-775-0708 or 800-541-7795.

DINING

Hemingway's Restaurant, on Route 4 south of Killington, is worth a trip to Vermont. Forget all the awards it's collected (we knew it way back when, and are happy to report that success has not gone to its head), and settle in to enjoy Vermont-raised game birds or succulent lamb prepared by a chef who treats each dish as though it were the only one he was preparing that evening. The atmosphere is a little more upscale than most ski-country dining rooms, but not stuffy or formal. For pure romance, ask for a table in the wine cellar. Do reserve well in advance; this is not an undiscovered place. The wine list is up to the menu's standards; 802-422-3886.

The Vermont Inn has a fieldstone fireplace in the dining room, which is lit by candles at dinner. Veal medallions are stuffed with spinach and cheddar, scallops sauteed with Dijon mustard and cream, with changing nightly specials; 802-775-0708.

The Killington access road is literally lined with restaurants and après ski places. These change rapidly, so for the best up-to-date advice, tell your innkeeper what you like and ask for directions.

MIDDLEBURY

A lively, but genteel college town, Middlebury is best known for its arts community and for the writers conference center at Bread Loaf, where such luminaries as Robert Frost spent summers. But not far from Bread Loaf, on one of the few year-round roads across the Green Mountains, is the Middlebury College Snow Bowl. It was built to serve the college and the community, but it is a favorite of laid-back skiers for its warm and friendly atmosphere, low-key facilities and good skiing. No weekend escapees from the city will cut in front of you in line as though their time were more important than yours, and if your kid falls down, some stranger (often a college student) will pick her up and dust her off.

The town itself is a nice place to be, with shops and restaurants catering to the college community as well as travelers.

FOR THOSE WHO SKI

Middlebury Snow Bowl joins Mad River Glen in its dedication to leaving the mountain shaped as nature left it, instead of creating new terrain. They are aided by the fact that nature seems to have designed the mountain with skiers in mind. We like the fact that beginners can find trails from the very top, and that easy trails don't lead skiers into those they can't handle. Lift rates are some of Vermont's lowest, with added deals for seniors and Vermont students. And if you'd like a quiet break, you'll find a library in the base lodge, where students and anyone else can catch up on reading. No glamour, no lines, no stress, just well-groomed trails for all ability levels, a friendly staff and great chili; 802-388-4356.

The **Ski Touring Center**, near the downhill area on Route 125, offers trails across the meadows and through the woodlands where Robert Frost spent many of his later summers writing. The college also lights a cross-country trail near the center of Middlebury, until 10 p.m.

OUTDOOR ACTIVITIES

Ice skating is available on the town rink, maintained by the Recreation Department; 802-388-4041.

INDOOR ACTIVITIES

The **Vermont Folklife Center** is just off the village green at One Park Street, encouraging the preservation of folklife traditions in Vermont and anywhere else. You can visit the exhibitions of folk art from Vermont and around the world on weekdays 9-5; 802-388-2117.

WHERE TO CURL UP BY THE FIRE

Several inns and B&Bs line Route 125 between the two ski areas and the intersection with Route 7, south of Middlebury. We like the **Chipman Inn**, in Ripton, with its fine antique architectural features and comfortable, non-fussy rooms. They serve dinners to guests on some nights, so be sure to ask when you reserve; 802-388-2390 or 800-890-2390.

For luxury, without formality, we travel a little farther from the Snow Bowl to **Brookside Meadows Country Bed & Breakfast**, a newly built inn in what looks like a country home. Spacious rooms were built to accommodate guests, with individual thermostats and good insulation for peace and quiet. Elegant furnishings invite you to spend some time there, as do the gregarious innkeepers, a couple who can tell you all about their area and suggest the best local chefs. You can ski or snowshoe on their 20 acres along a stream. Return from a day's skiing to relax with hosts over a glass of wine. Breakfasts are sumptuous; 802-388-6429 or 800-442-9887. They will give you directions, since it's on an unnumbered road.

DINING

The area's best-known restaurant is **Dog Team Tavern**, off Route 7 about four miles north of town. Traditional Yankee through and through, its menu features all the old favorites, all accompanied by the tavern's famous sticky buns. Dinner is served from 5-9 on Monday through Saturday, and from 12-9 on Sunday; 802-388-7651.

Stylish **Woody's**, overlooking Otter Creek from Bakery Lane (just past the theater), is forever finding new ways to work with seafood. Nightly specials may be based on cooking styles of Spain or France or farther afield, but will always be interesting and well-prepared. Lunch is served daily 11:30-3, dinner 5-10; 802-388-4182 or 800-346-3603.

For a quick, casual meal, step into **Neil & Otto's Pizza Cellar**, under the Baptist Church at 11 Merchant's Row. It will take a while to choose from the nearly overwhelming selection of pizzas starting at under $5. Open until 2 a.m.; 802-388-6774 or 388-6776.

THE MAD RIVER VALLEY

Here, Waitsfield and Warren share a valley and a way of life, and welcome skiers and travelers to share both with them. It's a real world of small town activities and hospitality, and it attracts those who enjoy simple country pleasures, in a setting of some sophistication and no little comfort. The excellent tourist facilities are a reminder of Sugarbush's origins with the high rollers, and the warmth is a testimony to the enduring fiber of a close-knit community. We enjoy both thoroughly.

For information on the area, its events, lodgings, activities and winter carnival, contact the Chamber of Commerce at 802-496-3409 or 800-82-VISIT.

FOR THOSE WHO SKI

Sugarbush, it is said, was where the phrase "Jet Set" originated. Once the darling of the moneyed international social crowd, it was left to the rest of us when they moved on to their next trendy venue. It has since become a favorite with serious and low-key skiers alike, for its friendly atmosphere, modern ski facilities and isolated location. 112 trails provide plenty of action for all abilities, even though half of them are at the intermediate level. A new top-of-the-mountain resort facility is underway; 802-583-2381, lodging 800-53-SUGAR.

Mad River Glen is a no-nonsense, no-frills area for serious skiers who care less about the facilities than about the challenge of the mountain. They get plenty of that on its 2000-foot vertical drop, among the highest in the state. It is the only ski area in America owned by the skiers. When its long-time and well-loved owner retired, skiers got together and bought it rather than have it become just another look-alike resort. They have retained the rigid policies of leaving the mountain's terrain in the shape nature intended, grooming trails as little as possible and banning snowboards. This is a place for skiers, not snow bunnies—no fancy lodge or après ski disco parties—but beginners needn't shun its friendly atmosphere. They will find separate trails and lift, and the security of knowing that trails remain true for their entire length. A beginner trail will not funnel skiers to a more advanced one; 802-496-3551.

The Round Barn on East Warren Road in Waitsfield has scenic cross-country trails and certified instructors, as well as equipment rentals; 802-496-6111. The **Sugarbush Nordic Center** has over 12 miles of groomed cross-country trails, with lessons and rentals at the Pavilion, opposite the Sugarbush Inn; 802-583-2381. **Blueberry Lake Cross Country Ski Center** (802-496-6687) and **Ole's Cross Country Center** (802-496-3430), both in Warren, have trails, rentals and instruction, as well.

OUTDOOR ACTIVITIES

Lareau Farm Country Inn, on Route 100 in Waitsfield, has a century-old three-passenger open sleigh that is used for **sleigh rides** through the woods to the Mad River, followed by hot cider. Rides are given by reservation on Friday, Saturday and Sunday afternoons, or by special appointment; 802-496-4949.

The Round Barn, an historic farm-turned-inn in Waitsfield, rents **snowshoes**, and is not exaggerating when it says their trails have the best views in the valley; 802-496-6111. **Clearwater Sports** on Route 100 in Waitsfield, offers snowshoe rentals and guided trips; 802-496-2708. The two co-sponsor an annual 8 km race in February, with food catered by American Flatbread Kitchen

Guided **snowshoe tours** on Vermont's Long Trail (a hiking trail that runs the length of the Green Mountains, from the Canadian border to the Massachusetts border) begin at Out Back at the Bush Center, located at the Lincoln Peak base area of Sugarbush. After a ride up the lift, participants traverse the trail between Lincoln Peak and Mount Ellen, a four-hour trip. The guide will lead the way and offer tips on the sport and point out features of the flora, fauna, geology and ecology of the winter woods; 802-583-2381.

Skating rinks are located at the Skatium in Waitsfield (802-496-9199), the pond in front of Mad River Flick, next to The Scoop Shop in Waitsfield, at Tucker's Plants on Route 100, and on the grounds of the elementary school in Warren; 802-496-2709. **Sugarbush Pavilion** has a rink where you can rent skates, or you can rent them from Inverness Ski Shop on Route 100; 802-496-3343.

Those who bring their own **snowmobile** will find more than 70 miles of groomed trails in the valley. This network is due to the work of VAST (see Snowmobiling in the *Introduction*), of which you must be a member if you plan to use the trails. You will also need to register your machine in Vermont, which you can do at Kenyon's Store in Waitsfield. The closest place to rent a snowmobile is Stowe.

Vermont Icelandic Horse Farm offers scenic trail rides on the world's most comfortable riding horses. These small gaited horses take riders on trails of several different lengths. Probably the most unusual sport in the valley is going for a "ride" on skis behind one of these horses. You can stay for a few days and take advantage of their packages that include room, meals and riding; 802-496-7141.

INDOOR ACTIVITIES

The **Sports Center** at Sugarbush offers resort guests heated pools, indoor tennis, a weight room, squash, racquetball, saunas and whirlpools; 802-583-2391.

CHRISTMAS CELEBRATIONS

December: **Sugarbush Country Christmas** lasts for the entire month, with caroling, concerts and a tree festival in the Joslyn Round Barn. Also at the Round Barn is a community carol sing, to which valley visitors and their children are welcome; 802-496-3409.

December: One evening during Christmas week, Sugarbush Resort holds their Holiday Celebration, with a torchlight parade, fireworks, and a party at the Gatehouse; 802-583-2381.

EVENTS

Late January: **Brookfield Ice Harvest:** Although as the crow flies, Brookfield is much closer to Warren than to Woodstock, the crow doesn't fly as well in winter. Since the shortest route goes straight up over a mountain and straight down the other side on a narrow winding road, you might prefer to drive north to I-89 and take it south to Brookfield; also see *Events* listing for *Woodstock* on page 62; 802-276-3959.

First week in February: **The Mad River Valley Winter Carnival** is a well-run celebration of winter that involves both local residents and visitors, bringing them together in a setting only Waitsfield and Warren could manage. Local restaurants (of which there are several outstanding ones) get involved, as does just about everyone, to provide a week of winter sports, cultural events, good food, ice sculpture, fireworks and activities for all ages, both indoors and out. More than 50 different events include an all-day free carnival for kids, with pony rides and puppet shows; 800-82-VISIT.

Mid-February: Sugarbush celebrates **Presidents Week** with a torchlight parade and fireworks, plus a dance band; 802-583-2381.

SHOPPING AND CRAFTS

Near the covered bridge in Warren is **Warren Village Pottery**, a studio and gallery shop filled with unique stoneware. Practical and decorative kitchen and tableware is made right there. The shop is open daily; 802-496-4162.

Waitsfield has a cluster of artists studios in the center of town, among them **Artisans' Gallery**, a showcase for emerging craftspeople and artists; 802-496-6256. **Waitsfield Pottery** is a showroom and gallery of functional stoneware in richly colored glazes and painted designs; 802-496-7155.

WHERE TO CURL UP BY THE FIRE

While the two towns have abundant inns of very high quality, our personal favorite is **The Inn at Round Barn Farm**. The barn itself, one of only a handful left in the state, is fascinating, and its owners have restored it for a variety of community uses, including a Christmas Tree festival, an art show, and the Sunday morning services of the local Episcopal parish. Rooms in the inn are well-designed for comfort, with stylish furniture, original art, whirlpool or steam baths, and fireplaces. Breakfast is unfailingly good and the public areas are well stocked with good books. The bottom line, however is the good humor and warmth of the engaging hosts, who are never too busy to chat with guests and help them plan their day in the valley. Inn guests can use the cross-country trails free; 802-496-2276.

Lareau Farm Country Inn is a comfortable farmhouse on Route 100 in Waitsfield. If your grandmother had lived on a Vermont farm, this would be it. Informal, comfortable, filled with the smells of good things in the oven and the hum of lively conversation, it has the camaraderie of a ski lodge and the warmth of a home. On the farm is the bakery/restaurant, **American Flatbread Kitchen**; 802-496-4949 or 800-833-0766.

The Inn at Mad River Barn is halfway between the slopes of Mad River Glen and Sugarbush, and offers 15 rooms and a dining room. Their in-house pub has a fireplace and guests are welcome to use the inn's snowshoes to wander in the surrounding woods and fields. The barn has the feel of a ski lodge from the early days of skiing, while the annex has more luxurious B&B rooms with steam baths; 802-496-3310 or 800-631-0466.

Sugarbush Village includes condos at the foot of the slope, townhouses and private mountain homes, many of which offer trailside access. A shuttle bus takes skiers to the slopes and non-skiers to the indoor sports facilities, restaurants and other places in the Sugarbush community. Attractively furnished and roomy, they have fully equipped kitchens and as many as five bedrooms; 800-451-4326.

Waterbury lodgings are not far away, especially **Grunberg Haus**, which is somewhat south of town on Route 100. See the *Stowe* section for lodging and dining suggestions in that area.

DINING

The Valley has more than 40 places to eat, so there are plenty of choices. **The Common Man Restaurant** is close to the slopes, in a well-converted 19th-century barn. Although the dining room is large, candlelight and small tables give it an intimate atmosphere and good service gives it polish. The menu is European, but not "continental stodgy"; for a hearty dinner after a day outdoors, order the bean cassoulet in a loaf of crusty bread. You will need reservations here; 802-583-2800.

At the Lareau Farm, **American Flatbread Kitchen** serves hearty meals at moderate prices on Friday and Saturday nights only; 802-496-8856.

Top places for the après ski scene are **The Blue Tooth** on the Sugarbush Access Road, **The Back Room** at Sugarbush South, **Mad Mountain Tavern** and **Gallagher's,** both at the junction of Routes 100 and 17 in Waitsfield. Live bands, DJs, Karaoke, pool tables, big screen TV, you'll find them at these nightspots; bring earplugs.

STOWE AND SMUGGLERS NOTCH

For dining, lodging, entertainment, social life and winter activities of all sorts, not very many people dispute that Stowe leads the other New England ski towns. Not everyone likes this ever-so-busy atmosphere, but whatever your dream of a winter vacation in New England is, you're likely to find it at Stowe. The town itself, for all the stir, is a lovely, white-churched, brick-inned setting, and the road toward the slopes has taken most of the pressure off the village center in building places to stay, play or dine. While there are certainly those who will tell you that Stowe has been ruined by all this success, it is the general consensus that the town has dealt well with the influx, and taken care to retain just those qualities that first made it attractive. There is an aura of class to most of Stowe's properties, and to the town itself; possibly because, through it all, Stowe *is* an active, operating Vermont town, with kids to educate, roads to plow and life to live.

Wise use of its land has been a high priority here, as has finding ways to accommodate the visitors without creating a towny-vs-tourist attitude. The solutions have benefited both. A case in point is the five-mile Stowe Recreation Path, which leads from the center of town along the river and up into Smugglers Notch. In the summer it is shared by walkers, runners, skaters and cyclists. In winter it becomes a track for cross-country skiers, winter walkers and snowshoers. Road crossings are well-marked, the path is paved and well-maintained, and it is heavily used, but it never loses its fresh quality, nor its involvement with the natural environment through which it passes. It is used by locals and visitors alike, and in all seasons, just as the town hoped it would be.

Amtrak stops in Waterbury on its New York to Montreal run, and most inns will arrange to pick you up from the station. For an Amtrak schedule, call 800-USA-RAIL; to avoid long telephone holding patterns, try late at night or in the early morning.

To check dates or get more information on the Stowe/ Waterbury area, contact the Stowe Area Association at 800-24-STOWE.

FOR THOSE WHO SKI

Smugglers Notch, on the opposite side of the notch from Stowe, is now connected to it by ski trails. The road over the notch is closed in the winter, so this ski-over-the-top feature at last makes it possible to ski in both areas on the same vacation without having to drive miles around the mountain. Its thousand acres of glades, woods and trails offer a wide variety of intermediate options, while its craggy face challenges experts; 802-644-8851 or 800-451-8752.

    Stowe Mountain is perhaps the best-known ski resort in Vermont, although not the largest The name has been synonymous with skiing since the early years of the sport's popularity. Nearly 60% of its trails are classed as intermediate; it offers less than many others for beginning skiers. 802-253-3000.

    Cross-country skiers will find abundant trails, from the Stowe Recreation Path that begins right in the village and parallels Mountain Road for five miles, to the **Trapp Family Lodge**; its more than 50 miles of trails include 60% carefully groomed and tended and 40% backcountry trails, perfect for those who like to explore on skis. Their ski school is among the best, too. The cross-country trails and center are open to the public; 802-253-8511 or 800-826-7000.

OUTDOOR ACTIVITIES

At least three attractions offer sleigh rides in the area. Those staying north of the notch will find **Vermont Horse Park** in Jeffersonville the most convenient. Their sleighs hold from four to sixteen passengers, with bench seats or hay. You will need advance reservations for their 45-minute rides, especially on moonlit nights, when the whole valley seems aglow. They also have daytime rides and horseback riding; 802-644-5347.

In nearby Morrisville, **Apple Cheek Farm** has a two-horse, 10-passenger open sleigh that you can ride through a forest lit with lanterns. Hot drinks and a farm tour are part of the ride; 802-888-4482.

In Stowe, both Topnotch Resort and Stoweflake Inn offer sleigh rides for their own guests and others. **Charlie Horse Sleigh and Carriage Rides** operate from Topnotch, with four one-horse sleighs, three bob sleighs and a Currier and Ives style sleigh that carries two adults and one child. Rides are offered daily, 11 a.m. to 4 p.m. from November 15 until March 1. **Sleigh driving lessons** are available, too. Evening rides for groups are by reservation only; 802-253-2215.

The Stowehof Inn on Edson Hill Road has two antique sleds from the Victorian era, which carry two adults and one child. These half-hour rides run during twilight and evening, 4-9 p.m. daily, and include a warm-up drink after the ride. This makes a nice evening when combined with dinner at the resort, and you can get both at a package price. Either way, you will need a reservation; 802-253-9722.

Trapp Family Lodge, a beautifully designed complex high on a ridge overlooking the snow-covered hills and valley, has some of the best cross-country skiing in the East, but offers equally fine **snowshoeing** terrain. Tucked around the property are several sites that give purpose to a hike on snowshoes: the sugarhouse, not far from the cross-country center, and the rustic stone Werner's Chapel are two, or you can snowshoe to the Austrian Tea Room for an afternoon strudel. We suggest snowshoeing to the Slayton Pasture Cabin, a weathered log cabin set on a hillside in the woods, about an hour's trip from the main lodge. It's uphill most of the way, but the nice thing about snowshoes is that you can stop as often as you like and walk at your own pace. The smoke rising from the chimney is from the fireplace, where you can warm up (you're not likely to get cold on the climb up) and have lunch. Hearty soups, sandwiches and the Trapp's famous Austrian pastries are on the menu, along with hot drinks. If you'd like to join a group, they offer guided trips, too; 802-253-8511 or 800-826-7000.

Skirack Outdoor Adventure School leads Sunday morning **snowshoe hikes** at the Ethan Allen Homestead in Burlington and the Catamount Family Center in Williston. Both are in beautiful locations and each offers a rich history, which you will learn about during the guided hike. You'll also learn to walk on snowshoes, but there's not much to learn if you already know how to walk without them. Tours and equipment cost only $10; 802-658-3313.

The **Green Mountain Club**, on Route 100, north of Waterbury, (802-244-7037) offers guided snowshoe walks, as does **Umiak Outdoor Outfitters**, which rents snowshoes and offers lessons as well; 802-253-2317 or 800-479-3380 (Vermont only). Umiak is on Route 100, south of the three-way stop in Stowe. **The Mountain Bike Shop**, on Mountain Road, rents snowshoes and offers guided snowshoe tours by appointment; 802-253-7919 or 800-MT-BIKE4.

Sledding is a popular activity on Sir Henry's Hill at Smugglers Notch.

Ice skating is available at the Jackson Arena in Stowe, where you can rent skates; 802-253-6148. Skates may also be rented at the outdoor rink at the Smugglers Notch Nordic Ski Center.

Ice fishing is not an easy sport to "try out" since it requires a bobhouse for shelter, but Smugglers Notch offers guests a one-day ice fishing trip complete with transportation, heated bobhouse, fishing equipment, and hot cocoa. If you're over 15 years old, you'll need a fishing license, which costs only $7; 802-644-8851.

To rent snowmobiles in the Stowe area, which includes the use of their trails, contact **Nichols Snowmobile Rentals** in Stowe; 802-253-7239.

After a hiatus, the **Trapp Family Lodge** reopened the sugarhouse that was built in the 1950s, when the family first began to tap the maples in the woods behind the lodge. They now tap 1000 trees in the traditional way, and gather all the sap on sleighs pulled by their team of Belgian horses. Lodge guests are invited to join in the activity, and non-guests are welcome to visit the sugarhouse and watch the boiling process from a gallery that gives them a close look. You can get to the sugarhouse on skis, snowshoes or by sleigh.

The von Trapps insist on a self-sustaining approach to sugaring; they use buckets instead of plastic tubing, horses help to collect the sap, and the wood that fuels the evaporator is gathered when the lodge thins their sugarbush each fall. It is one of the few places where this traditional method is really used, although some others have a few trees to show visitors how it used to be done. On Saturday afternoons they have sugar-on-snow parties, and special weekend packages for families during sugar season; 802-253-8511 or 800-826-7000.

Nebraska Knoll Sugarhouse has 4000 taps on a steep hillside, and arranges sugaring parties. Visitors are welcome to watch the boiling process at the sugarhouse; 802-253-4655.

At Lake Elmore, north of Stowe, **Elmore Sugar House** has a sugaring video for visitors, and a store with a variety of Vermont-made products. They also arrange sugaring parties; 802-888-7890.

In Huntington, **Green Mountain Audubon Nature Center** has free sugaring parties on Sunday afternoons in March. Their exhibits and demonstrations explore the history of maple production, including how Native Americans boiled sap. You can watch the sugaring operation daily and follow a self-guided trail at their sugarhouse; 802-434-3068.

Stop at the information office in Stowe for a copy of the **Walking Tour of the Historic District**, and find some of the architectural gems as well as fascinating tidbits of history. This way, you'll know just where to look for the bullet hole that still marks the front of Shaw's General Store and which house served as a station on the Underground Railroad.

Indoor Activities

During the month of December and the first week of January, the Helen Day Art Center in Stowe is filled with beautifully decorated trees in the **Annual Festival of Christmas Trees.** These original creations are the work of local designers, decorators, artists and others who love the opportunity to dress trees for the season. The Helen Day Center is one block off the main street (Route 100), in the center of the village. 802-253-8358.

Craft classes are offered by local artists at Smugglers Notch and include painting, dried flower arranging, beading, tin punching and several stenciling techniques; 802-644-8851.

The **Trapp Family Lodge** has a full activity program that includes lessons and workshops in painting, calligraphy and flower arranging. While guests have first dibs, these workshops are open to non-guests on a standby basis. The once-weekly baking class with the Lodge's pastry chef is almost certain to be filled by guests, so it's wise to sign up early even if you're staying there; 802-253-8511 or 800-826-7000.

Montpelier, the smallest state capital in the country, is a very pleasant town for browsing, dining, admiring the fine architecture, or just hanging out in a cafe. The **State House** is an imposing granite building with marble floors, spiral stairs and fine carved wooden ornamentation. Exhibits include historic flags and a gallery of Vermont artists in the hallway outside the governor's office. The building is open Monday through Friday, 8 a.m.-4 p.m., and free tours are occasionally offered; 802-828-2228.

The **Vermont Historical Society**, next door to the State House, has exhibits as well as an excellent library where you can read about any facet of life in the state, or research your own Vermont roots. It's open Tuesday through Sunday; 802-828-2291.

The **Ben & Jerry's Ice Cream** factory, just north of Waterbury on Route 100, is one of Vermont's top tourist attractions. Along with a guided tour, you can see a video and get a sample of their famous ice cream; 802-244-TOUR.

The **Waterbury Village Library**, just a few doors from The Old Stagecoach Inn on Route 10, has a charming little museum filled with an unpredictable assortment of antique furniture, memorabilia and old photographs. Especially interesting are the photos and accounts of the 1927 flood, when the entire downtown was under water. The World War II era is represented with such items as condensed versions of *Time* and *The New Yorker* that were published and sent to the troops overseas. Doll collectors will be interested in the handmade dolls representing different eras of American history. The museum is free, and open during library hours.

CHRISTMAS CELEBRATIONS

December (usually the third week): Stowe's **Sounds of Christmas** celebrates the season with musical events, a skating party, sleigh rides and caroling.

December 24: Smugglers Notch Resort celebrates the holiday with a **Christmas Eve Spectacular**. Santa arrives across the ski slopes, everyone sings carols, enjoys refreshments and joins in a non-denominational candlelight service; 802-644-8851.

EVENTS

Early January: **Lake Elmore Dog Sled Races**, north of Stowe, brings mushers of all ages—even preschoolers—from all over New England to compete. There is no admission charge, and spectators can be sure of a lively show; call 800-24-STOWE for the exact dates.

End of January to early February: **Stowe Winter Carnival** is the model other places have used to design theirs. It's an extravaganza of winter activities, indoors and out, with an accent on active sports, but plenty of après ski and events for everyone. Activities include ice sculpting, sled dog races and snowshoe races. In past years one of the most hilarious events has been an **ice bowling contest using frozen turkeys** as bowling balls; 800-24-STOWE.

Early March: **Town Meeting Day** is observed all over Vermont, but in Waterbury it is the occasion for eating as well as voting. At the Elementary School a potluck luncheon is served at noon (802-244-7371) and from 5 to 7 in the evening, an all-you-can-eat supper is served at the Grange Hall in Waterbury Center; 802-244-7371. If you have never been to a New England town meeting, choose a small town and stop in for a spell. Nearly every town hall has a visitor's gallery or a few rows in the back reserved for non-voters.

Easter: **A Sunrise Service and Children's Celebration** atop Vermont's highest peak is held outside Cliff House, and followed by an Easter Egg hunt.

A Spa Retreat

You don't have to have tired muscles after a day on Mount Mansfield's trails to treat yourself to the luxury of a spa. In fact we've never needed any excuse at all at **Topnotch Resort and Spa**, on Mountain Road in Stowe, especially when their hydro-massage involves sitting under a waterfall in a landscaped indoor pool. Massages, herbal wraps, beauty, fitness and aerobics instruction, and general pampering of the body and mind are their specialties and winter is the best time to enjoy them. It's a full service resort, with spa cuisine so tasty you'll forget it's good for you; 802-253-8585 or 800-451-8686 or reserve along with other New England lodgings through 800-333-INNS.

All-in-One Resorts

In the self-contained environment of **Smugglers Notch**, all activities, from skiing to sing-alongs for the whole family, are located within a small area. Family activities, such as Karaoke, bingo, games and sleigh rides, take place after the lifts close and last until mid-evening. Adult entertainment begins at 9 p.m. with a comedy club and more Karaoke. A teen center is open from 4 to 11 p.m. with games, a DJ, videos, snacks, and pool table. Sports include ice skating, snowshoe tours and trails, volleyball, water basketball, tennis, swimming and snow soccer, and after-sports facilities offer saunas, hot tubs, massage, and other pampering. Owling tours, craft lessons, bonfires with hot cocoa, and a Breakfast with the Chef program are all within walking distance of your accommodations. Tune in to the in-house TV channel for the latest schedule of activities; 800-451-8752.

SHOPPING AND CRAFTS

Locally-produced foods are the specialty of **Vermont Maple Outlet** in Jeffersonville, although they have a fair selection of crafts as well. Maple, of course, reigns supreme, with Vermont cheeses, cob-smoked meats and other goodies filling the shelves. They are on Route 15; 802-644-5482.

In Stowe, on Route 100 at the Lower Village, **Dia Jenks** knits sweaters from cotton, wool and chenille, based on traditional Estonian and American designs. The shop is open Monday through Saturday from 10:30 a.m. to 5:30 p.m., and Sundays from 1-5 p.m.; 802-253-9784.

On Moscow Road, a less busy approach to the mountain, you'll find **Little River Hotglass Studio**, where you can watch Michael Trimpol create stunning art glass bottles, eggs, balls and goblets. His perfume bottles are characterized by their clean lines and vivid colors, and by the contrasting use of thick clear glass bases that flow into delicately turned collars at the upper rims. Visitors are welcome to the studio, and to the adjoining showroom on Thursday through Monday, 10 a.m. to 5 p.m.; 802-253-0889. Next door is **Highland Pottery Studio**, where the work of several potters, including Jaime McCutcheon, are shown and sold. It is also a working studio, where you can watch works in progress 10-5 daily; 802-253-2339.

Stowe Forge and Stone Works, on Mountain Road, shows the fanciful and diverse metal sculptures of Chris LeBaron. Using sheet steel, brass and copper, he creates everything from candlesticks to life-sized sculptures of water birds. Visit the studio 8:30-5 Monday through Friday; 802-253-7625.

Bear Pond Books packs a lot of titles into a small space, and still leaves room for comfortable browsing. In the depot building in the center of Stowe, it's open daily from 9-6 and sometimes later; 802-253-8236.

Cabot Annex Store, on Route 100 in Waterbury Center, can't provide you with a factory tour in person, as the dairy in Cabot does, but they do show the process on a video and offer samples of their cheeses. The shop carries other Vermont specialty foods, too; 802-244-6334. Sharing the building is **Green Mountain Chocolate Company**, with over 100 varieties of chocolates; 802-244-1139.

Also in the village of Waterbury Center, **Cold Hollow Cider Mill** demonstrates cider pressing year-round, and offers free samples. Its large retail shop sells Vermont specialty foods, baked goods, and Vermont products. It's wheelchair accessible; 802-244-8771 or 800-3-APPLES.

In the same area is **Ziemke Glassblowing Studio**, where you can watch vases, goblets, perfume bottles and paperweights created from molten lumps of glass. Demonstrations are Thursday-Monday, but the showroom at the studio is open daily from 10-6; 802-244-6126.

Vermont Windtoys creates whirligigs in folk art styles for indoor or outdoor use; 802-244-8940.

WHERE TO CURL UP BY THE FIRE

Butternut Inn at Stowe is a B&B with lots of extras. Afternoon tea includes soup or stew by the fireside and is complimentary to the inn's guests. Snowshoe trails are lighted. It is not a place for children since antiques abound; 802-253-4277 or 800-3-BUTTER.

There is an almost indefinable air of hospitality about **The Gables Inn**, which you feel the minute you walk in. It isn't frilly and it isn't pretentious, but you immediately feel at home there. It's largely due to its resident owners, who know every one of their guests. All the extras are here—fireplaces, whirlpools, a good restaurant, outdoor hot tub, bountiful breakfasts—and it is only a few yards from Stowe's exceptional walking/skiing/snowshoeing path. 802-253-7730 or 800-GABLES-1.

The **Green Mountain Inn** is a classic. Its corridors wind and curve as they lead to a charming assortment of architectural nooks and crannies and rooms set into gables. The modern amenities are all there, including whirlpool tubs, hair dryers, air conditioning and in-room phones, but in such a charmingly old-fashioned setting you really do feel like you've stepped back into the Stowe of a century ago. Antiques and a collection of local art decorate the halls and public areas. Warm-from-the-oven cookies are served with cider or tea every afternoon in the front parlor, where you can also find complimentary coffee after dinner, or you can retire to the complimentary health club in the rear wing of the inn. Its location, right on Stowe's main street, is convenient for skiers and non-skiers alike, since a trolley runs from the door to the slopes and Stowe's varied assortment of fine shops also surround the inn. You can walk to several good restaurants, or dine in. Special winter packages include a snowshoe picnic or a winter afternoon sleigh ride—or both. As you may have guessed, we always enjoy staying here; 802-253-7301 or 800-253-7302.

Grunberg Haus, just south of Waterbury on Route 100, is a rambling chalet with the architectural quirks we love (have you noticed that we rarely rave about a place with straight corridors?). Rich wood tones predominate, which accentuates the general feeling of coziness and warmth. The innkeepers are congenial and helpful, and it's the kind of inn where everyone gathers in the comfortable couches at the end of the day to compare notes. The outdoor hot tub, a room with a Dutch cabinet bed, antique furnishings, the elegantly served hearty breakfasts, and the innkeeper's piano playing are the frosting. On the hillside above the inn are several newly-built cabins perfect for privacy. You can't drive a car to them, but they are on a cross-country trail, so you can ski or snowshoe home. Guests are invited to use the inn's snowshoes without charge. And speaking of charges, the rates begin at $60 for two, including breakfast; 800-800-7760.

In the center of downtown Waterbury (don't picture a noisy Main Street atmosphere here) **The Old Stagecoach Inn** looks exactly like what it is, with its wrap-around porches and general air of hospitality. The rooms are individually decorated, each in keeping with its architecture; we like the third-floor rooms: though they don't have the antiques of the others, they're so bright and airy with their skylights. One room has a much-noticed ghost. The owners have an easy tongue-in-cheek humor that makes guests instantly feel at home; they are also good chefs. Children are welcome. It is only half a mile from exit 10 of I-91; 802-244-5056 or 800-262-2206.

North of Waterbury, on Route 100, **The Black Locust Inn** is a classy B&B in an early 1800s farmhouse. Rooms are individually decorated in antiques and common rooms have plenty of places to curl up with a good book. They offer guests complimentary use of snowshoes to explore the surrounding woods and fields; 802-244-7490 or 800-366-5592.

Stowehof Inn is perched on a mountainside amid sloping meadows, and on-site sleigh rides earn it resort status, but the feeling is pure inn. Its sunken hearth, where everyone gathers for après ski snacks, is in a large window-enclosed common room broken into comfortable sitting areas with alcoves for games or curling up with a book, although the distraction of the mountain views might be too great for concentration; 802-253-9722 or 800-932-7136.

When someone suggests to us that a resort offers so much to do that you never need to leave it, we smile politely and think our own thoughts. But the **Trapp Family Lodge** really *did* keep us occupied when we stayed there.

We divided our outdoor time between skiing the cross-country trails and exploring the property on snowshoes. We rode to the little Austrian tearoom in a sleigh. We listened to harp music, ate warm cookies, studied the delicately detailed original illustrations for a book on the von Trapp family, and we had wienerschnitzel for dinner. It is a beautiful place, Tyrolean in architecture with balconies and handcarved balustrades, and although you never forget the remarkable family that built it, they never get too schmaltzy or tiresome by overplaying the theme. The sound of music is still in the air, with Sunday morning coffee concerts, and live harp music in the dining room every night. You can even take harp lessons during your stay there. Winter packages offer lower rates: a four-night Thanksgiving or two-night pre-Christmas break include a fresh-cut Christmas tree, and "Tap at the Trapps" adds sugaring activities and syrup to sweeten the deal; 802-253-8511 or 800-826-7000.

Ye Olde England Inne on Mountain Road in Stowe, offers a slightly different ambiance, with afternoon tea served to guests in the setting of a fine English country inn. Rooms have canopy or cannonball four-poster beds, Laura Ashley decor, many have Jacuzzi tubs and some have fireplaces. Pre-Christmas packages (early November to mid-December) include a choose-and-cut-your-own Christmas tree. Rates begin at about $120 a night for two; 802-253-7558.

Those who prefer the intimacy and special hospitality of a small B&B in a family home will love **Tibbits House**, set on 21 acres of rolling meadow and forest in Stowe. You can snowshoe or cross-country ski out the back door, but you won't want to hurry away from the warmth of the big woodstove in the kitchen where your breakfast is prepared. Quilts, antiques, and the warm atmosphere of being house guests in a country home make this an unusually pleasant place to get away from it all; 802-253-4770.

Montpelier is close enough to the winter activities of Stowe and Waterbury—to which it is connected via a short drive down I-89—so you still feel you're having a winter vacation, but offers its own historical and architectural attractions. Our pick is **The Inn at Montpelier**, a comfortably elegant inn on a residential street in the heart of town. It is an easy walk to shops and restaurants—there's an excellent dining room in the inn itself—and the Statehouse; 802-223-2727.

The Jefferson House, on Main Street in Jeffersonville, is a warm Victorian home with hearty homestyle breakfasts and budget-friendly rates, especially for the area; 802-644-2030 or 800-253-9630.

With comfortable, tidy cabins that are nestled in the snow-covered woods, **1836 Cabins** make a cozy retreat where you can do your own cooking and ski or snowshoe right out your own front door. They even furnish free snowshoes. Located off Route 100, close to the Green Mountain Club, the cabins sleep four or six persons; some have gas fireplaces, and the kitchens are fully equipped; 802-244-8533.

DINING

For a good overview of comparative restaurant prices in the area, get a copy of *The Stowe Guide and Magazine* and turn to their *What's on the Menu?* page.

We admit right up front that chef-owned **Villa Tragara Ristorante**, north of Waterbury on Route 100, is one of our all-time favorite restaurants. We not only eat unfailingly good food there, but the service is always informed and lively, the hospitality warm, and the atmosphere just right for a relaxed, congenial evening. Rarely do we encounter a staff so knowledgeable about fine foods and wine; in fact, we've learned about some of Vermont's best little-known restaurants from our conversations with them. Plan a leisurely evening, with time to savor everything from the antipasto (order the combination plate if it is on the menu) to the desserts— which you should not even think of skipping. This is one of those rare restaurants where we ask the waiter to bring us "whatever Tony likes best tonight." (Once it was veal scaloppine wrapped around a stuffing of sausage, pine nuts, broccoli and raisins, in a sherry sauce.) Reserve ahead: we're not the only ones who think this place is great; 802-244-5288.

Blue Moon Cafe in Stowe is small and intimate, but tables are well-spaced in a Tuscan atmosphere. Begin with crabcakes—pure crab with no fillers—served on grilled Vidalia onion slices with a green salsa cream. Wines are reasonably priced, with several good choices in the $15 range. Don't look here for "Wow, how did they ever come up with that combination?" entrees, but the menu is far from a ho-hum list, with butterflied lamb chops, chili-encrusted soft shell crabs, halibut grilled with Venetian red bean sauce and chicken and wild local mushroom ragout, each dish a nice blend of flavors and textures. Open daily from 6-9:30 p.m.; 802-253-7006.

You should plan a meal at **The Whip Bar and Grill** in the Green Mountain Inn, just to read the menu. Don't get us wrong: the food is very good, too, but the menu is filled with old photographs of Stowe, including long-ago hotels, a huge livery barn, the Mount Mansfield Stage, the electric railroad, and more. Start with their signature corn chowder, then choose from grilled chicken marinated in tequila and lime, sesame-encrusted salmon, or shepherd's pie baked in a giant potato. Vegetarian and heart-healthy selections abound. Then savor the old photos and their captions; 802-253-7301.

Isle de France, on Mountain Road in Stowe is an institution in these parts, serving French classics in two different atmospheres. Claudine's is a casual bistro while their elegant dining room is more formal. As you would expect, the wine list is outstanding. Serving dinner daily from 6-10 p.m.; 802-253-7751.

McCarthy's, also on Mountain Road, is a breakfast favorite for locals, where you can also get a good healthy lunch. They have special menus for kids along with low-fat and low-cholesterol items. They open at 6:30 a.m. and close at 3 p.m.; 802-253-8626.

The Shed, on Mountain Road near the intersection of Luce Road, was a local standby for many years before it was destroyed by fire. Back again, this time with a lively microbrewery, it offers pub food and hearty steaks, chicken and seafood dishes, with six ales on tap. The pub opens at noon. They give brewery tours, too; 802-253-4765.

Miguel's Stowe Away bills itself as a "Mexican restaurant and cantina" and serves creative dishes inspired by the ingredients and cooking styles of Mexico. They do it very well—we especially liked the crabmeat enchiladas—and for very reasonable prices. Like most everything else in town, they are on Mountain Road Miguel's is open 11:30-3:30 for lunch and 5:30-10 for dinner; 802-253-7574.

Trattoria La Festa is very service oriented, offering well-prepared predictable Italian specialties in the warm atmosphere of a family-run trattoria. They are open only for dinner from 5-10 daily; 802-253-8480.

Tanglewoods, just off the I-89 interchange in Waterbury, takes food and its preparation very seriously, with a menu that ranges from sesame-coriander encrusted tuna steak to sirloin steak in bourbon sauce. Or you might find sea scallops sauteed with hickory cured mushrooms, leeks and roasted red peppers. A cafe menu offers lighter fare, from the chef's daily pizzetta creation to potstickers with a ginger dipping sauce. We've never been disappointed in this chef-owned restaurant. Open Tuesday through Saturday from 5:30-10, and reservations are a must; 802-244-7855.

Pickwick's, in **Ye Olde England Inne**, offers a good menu rich in game meats, including venison, wild boar and partridge, along with 150 ales from all over the world, Scottish single malts, rare cognacs and vintage ports; 802-253-7558.

Start the day right with a hearty breakfast at **The Gables Inn**, even if you are not staying there. If you aren't skiing, we suggest you wait until the skiers have bolted their bacon and eggs and rushed off for the first morning run, then settle in for a nice, relaxed encounter with a Green Mountain Omelet, Belgian waffles with Ben & Jerry's ice cream, kippers with onions, sauteed chicken livers or a Nova Scotia lox and bagel plate; the latter is the most expensive thing on the menu and it's only $7.95. Heart-healthy choices are listed, or the chef will adapt almost any other entree for you; 802-253-7730.

The only problem with **Whiskers Restaurant** in the winter is that their spectacular gardens are covered with snow. Maybe it's better, since without the gardens as a distraction, you can give full attention to your hot cheesecake or chocolate raspberry torte. With desserts like those, it's harder to remember the main course, but we do recall sweet potato fries with aioli and delicious crabcakes with hush puppies. The truly ambitious will arrive on snowshoes, via the Stowe Recreation Path, which runs right past the back gate. Whiskers is also very popular for its après ski conviviality; 802-253-8996.

In the center of Waterbury, look for **Arvad's**, a good place to stop for lunch or an informal dinner. You can also get an espresso or cappuccino and a serving of pastry from their in-house bakery for an afternoon pick-you-up. We particularly like their hummus sandwich on oatmeal bread and the jalapenos stuffed with Vermont cheddar; those will warm you right up on a cold day; 802-244-8973.

Burke Mountain
and the Northeast Kingdom

East Burke—home of Burke Mountain—gathers around its general store and a classic white steepled church. It's the kind of village that ski areas farther south would have used to model their new buildings after since it looks like a ski town should, except that its motif is pure New England, not Tyrolean. It's prime snowmobile country, with one of the major VAST trails passing through the center of town (the refueling stop is at the town's single gas pump.) With all this rusticity, it is closer to an Interstate exit than most other New England ski areas, only 7 miles from I-91.

For information on the Northeast Kingdom, contact the Lyndon Area Chamber of Commerce, P.O. Box 886, Lyndonville, VT 05851; 802-626-9696.

For Those Who Ski

Burke Mountain is a friendly resort favored by families and intermediate skiers, although it has trails in all ranges. It is one of the few that offers a novice trail from the top, but its terrain is challenging enough to provide a training ground for U.S. Olympic Team skiers. It has the low-key atmosphere of a local ski area, but its facilities are nice enough to attract traveling skiers. Burke is in the Northeast Kingdom, about 15 miles north of St. Johnsbury; 802-626-3305.

The Burke Cross Country Ski Area spans maple, birch and spruce forests and rolling meadows with 50 miles of trails. The center is right at the ski area, which makes it handy for families with divided interests; 802-626-8338 or 800-786-8383.

Craftsbury Outdoor Center in Craftsbury Common is a full-service cross-country ski resort, with more than 60 miles of trails, lodging and hearty meals; 802-586-2514 or 800-729-7751.

OUTDOOR ACTIVITIES

Although the entire state is webbed with well-maintained "white highways" for snowmobilers, Island Pond, in the Northeast Kingdom, is the **snowmobile** capital of the state. Surrounded by frozen lakes, a state park and miles of wilderness, Island Pond is ideally situated. For guided tours on your own snowmobile, including tours that go across the border into Canada, contact **Barnes Recreation**, RR 1, Box 194, Island Pond 05846; 802-723-6331 (between 6 and 9 p.m.).

Ice skating is available in Lyndon Center, at the Fenton Chester Arena, where you can also rent skates; 802-626-9361. Outdoor skating on a well-tended pond is found in Craftsbury, at the Craftsbury Outdoor Center; 802-586-7767.

Snowshoe trails are also part of the Craftsbury Outdoor Center complex.

For **sleigh rides** its hard to beat the landscapes of the Northeast Kingdom, and the Wildflower Inn in Lyndonville has chosen some of the loveliest of them for its hilltop setting. Their 15-passenger sled is drawn by Belgian draft horses for a 30-40 minute ride across their property, where you can look down into the valley and out across the other hills. The Inn is on Darling Hill Road in Lyndonville; 802-626-8310 or 800-627-8310.

Laplant's Sugar House, in addition to running an old-fashioned thousand-bucket sugarbush, gives sleigh rides with their team of Belgians. Day and evening rides end with a warm-up snack and a cup of hot cocoa or cider. Because they are so busy during sugaring season, they do not give rides at that time, but invite you to visit the sugarbush and sample some syrup between 9 a.m. and 5 p.m. They are in Sutton, three miles north of West Burke on Route 5; 802-467-3900.

Lake Willoughby is a favorite spot for **ice fishing**, and few settings offer as scenic a backyard for your bobhouse. **Snowmobile** trails crisscross the lake and the surrounding meadows, even the steep mountainsides that rise directly from its shore. This deep glacier-carved lake and its flanking mountains form the dramatic scoop in the skyline that you can see from the summit of Burke Mountain; the lake is often compared to a fjord for its depth and mountain walls.

All Around Power in St. Johnsbury has snowmobile rentals; 802-748-1413.

Walk through the winter woods to the historic sugarhouse at **Sugar Ridge Farm**, in St. Johnsbury, where you can see how sap is boiled into syrup by modern methods; 802-748-2318.

INDOOR ACTIVITIES

If you love the look, feel and smell of Victorian museums as much as we do, you'll find the **Fairbanks Museum and Planetarium** in St. Johnsbury irresistible. The building itself is a treasure, with its polished wood cabinets and balcony surrounding the upper reaches of the main exhibit hall. The collections—the largest natural history collections north of Harvard—also include a charming assemblage of cultural and ethnographic material from Asia, Africa and elsewhere, collected and neatly (although sometimes puzzlingly) labeled by Victorian travelers. Don't miss the original snowflake photographs by the Vermonter who invented the technique of recording the crystals on film. Downstairs is the U.S. Weather Station, whence Mark Breen brings "Eye on the Sky" to Vermonters each morning. The planetarium is excellent, as well; 802-748-2372.

Also in St. Johnsbury, **Maple Grove Farms** started over 80 years ago when two women began making maple confections in their family farm kitchen; it is now the largest manufacturer of maple candies in the world. Tours of their factory are offered on weekdays, and the sugarhouse museum follows the tapping, gathering and boiling process, with examples of historic equipment on display. Open 8-5 daily, weekdays only after Christmas; 802-748-5141.

Trout River Brewing Company in East Burke, right behind Bailey's Country Store, produces bitters, stouts and reds, all uncommonly good. Sample them on a brewery tour. Open 7 a.m. to 7 p.m. from Monday through Thursday, 12-8 Friday and Saturday, and 1-5 on Sunday; 802-626-3984 or 800-BYO-BREW.

EVENTS

Christmas Week: Children have a chance to go for a **sleigh ride with Santa**, and adults look forward to Santa's Elves' Dance during the holidays; 802-626-3305.

New Years Eve: A traditional **Torchlight Parade** brings members of the Burke Mountain staff down the trails with lighted torches. A dinner and dance at the base lodge follows; 802-626-3305.

Early January: **Northeast Kingdom Sled Dog Races** begin at Wildflower Inn in Lyndonville; 802-626-8310.

February: **Inter-Mountain Snowshoe Obstacle Race**, with snowshoe competitions between the ski staff of several ski areas; 802-626-3305.

Late March: **Burke Mountain Sugaring Celebration**, with maple treats and ski events for all abilities; 802-626-3305.

SHOPPING AND CRAFTS

Heirloom comforters filled with fluffy warm goose down raised in the Northeast Kingdom are the specialty at **Highland Duvet** in Lyndonville; 802-626-8091.

Bailey's Country Store in East Burke carries country

gifts, woodenware and Vermont food products; 802-626-3666.

In St. Johnsbury, look for **The Northern Lights Bookshop**, which carries an excellent selection of books on Vermont, including some not easily found. They also have a cafe, with good scones and a choice of real teas, as well as a full breakfast and lunch menu; 802-748-4463.

WHERE TO CURL UP BY THE FIRE

The Wildflower Inn has one of the finest settings of any in Vermont, high on a ridge with sweeping views across the valley and mountains. In the summer, its flower gardens are stunning, but we shouldn't mention that now. The owners, tired of searching for nice places to stay that welcomed children, decided to create their own, and it's just as they'd planned it. Parents—and a good number of adults without children—can enjoy the pleasures of a fine inn and dining room, while kids can find plenty to do, and aren't forever being shooed out of something. They'll enjoy the petting barn, game rooms, and a child-welcoming atmosphere. Sleigh rides and snowshoe trails and ice skating keep the non-skier entertained and skiers are only a few minutes from the slopes: cross-country trails leave from the door. The hot tub and sauna take care of the tired muscles afterward. The dining room offers meals kids will love, without sacrificing the cuisine adults travel for. Take Darling Hill Road from Route 5 just north of the center of Lyndonville; 802-626-8310 or 800-627-8310.

Inn at Mountain View, The Creamery, is an historic inn with ten rooms and cross-country trails leading from the backyard; 802-626-9924 or 800-572-4509.

Rabbit Hill Inn, in Lower Waterford, recreates a world that never was, but which sybaritic travelers want to believe in. And while you're there it *does* exist. Fireplaces, lace, canopied beds, whirlpools in some rooms, it's ambiance with a capital *A*. And if you need to breathe the crisp Vermont air, you can do it on snowshoes or a toboggan on their extensive property; 802-748-5168 or 800-76-BUNNY.

Overlooking Lake Willoughby (whose scenic attractions are described above, under *Outdoor Activities*) is **The WilloughVale Inn**, with views from each of its seven unique rooms and four lakefront cottages. The guest rooms have handcrafted Vermont furniture. A casual Tap Room offers après ski food and drink, while the main dining room offers lake views and a more formal setting; 802-525-4123.

Snowmobilers heading for Island Pond will want to stay at the **Lakefront Motel**, a nicely kept property where snowmobile fans gather. Its owner, an avid VAST member, knows everything that's going on in the area, as well as the trails you'll be riding; 802-723-6507.

Burke Mountain Northern Star has 69 condo units at the mountain, with woodburning stoves or fireplaces; 802-626-8903 or 800-541-5480.

Information on local B&B accommodations is available at 800-377-1212.

DINING

Dinner at the **Wildflower Inn** might begin with a turkey cashew pate before moving on to veal saltimbocca over spinach fettuccine or chicken braised with honey and lemon. Desserts, priced below $3, include a chocolate fondue of fresh fruit or raspberry pie. The setting is so lovely you'll want to arrive early and watch the sunset over the mountains; 802-626-8310.

River Garden Cafe in East Burke serves lunch and dinner in an upbeat, bright atmosphere. The menu features smoked Vermont trout bruschetta, filled chicken and pasta dishes; 802-626-3514.

Miss Lyndonville Diner is pure nostalgia, with good reliable food as a bonus. Roast turkey, liver and onions, baked fresh haddock, hot turkey sandwich, a three-decker club...you get the idea. No frills, no rosemary trees stuck in your meat, no pasta-fad-of-the-month. It's a diner and it always will be, but they will use egg substitutes in your omelet if you ask. The diner is on Route 5 and is open daily from 6 a.m. until 9 p.m.; 802-626-9890.

JAY PEAK

The town of Montgomery, with its two separate village centers, was a thriving logging center in the middle 1800s, but like many other upcountry towns, couldn't compete with towns nearer the transportation routes leading to their markets. The development of Jay Peak has been a godsend to the town's economy, sparking second homes and resorts and bringing tourism to Montgomery. It's a fairly recent change, and it has brought new stores, inns, B&Bs and hotels. But Montgomery's distance from the major eastern U.S. cities means that the region is seldom crowded.

Montgomery is not a gentrified boutique town, although it has all the amenities. Each one of these tidy B&Bs, shops and restaurants has grown the hard way, with a lot of work by gritty people who were determined to survive in a town they liked. It isn't Stowe, and it doesn't want to be.

The white columned facade of the Baptist Church at the head of Main Street, built in 1866 when the town was thriving and prosperous, is decorated at Christmas with a twenty-foot wreath (pine boughs are plentiful in the north country) and lighted to serve as the focal point of the town's festivities.

FOR THOSE WHO SKI

Jay Peak is a stone's throw from Canada, which accounts for its distinctly Quebecoise atmosphere; you'll hear more French spoken there than English. It is also a favorite for backcountry and adventurous skiers, with 18 glades, two chutes and hundreds of acres of off-trail skiing. Jay has a vertical rise of over 2,100 feet and over 50 trails. It consistently records the highest natural snowfall of any ski area in the east, often over 300 inches in a single season; 802-988-2611 or 800-451-4449.

Hazen's Notch Cross Country Ski Area, on Route 58 on the way to Hazen's Notch, with more than 15 miles of groomed trails and 70 miles of backcountry trails, provides good conditions even when southern areas have little snow; 802-326-4708.

OUTDOOR ACTIVITIES

Rose Apple Acres Farm, a B&B on East Hill Road in North Troy, has an antique two-passenger one-horse sleigh and a larger sleigh that carries 12 passengers, which they use for 30-minute sleigh rides, adding hot cider or chocolate afterward. In case there isn't enough snow, they use a wagon as a backup. Reservations are required for both the large and small sleighs; 802-988-2503.

Weekly **snowshoe walks** are led by a staff naturalist for guests at Jay Peak Resort. Snowshoes are available for rent, with plenty of cross-country trails and logging roads in the area. The resort also has a rink for **ice skating**, lighted for evening use. Skate rentals and broomball equipment are available.

Resort guests can also take part in a weekly schedule of activities, including rides on the **snow cats** (snow grooming machines) each Tuesday and trips to a working **dairy farm** on Wednesdays and an evening **sledding** party with a campfire and marshmallow roast. Special programs for teens include snow volleyball, movie and bowling nights, skating parties, and dances; 802-988-2611 or 800-451-4449.

Godfrey's Sugarhouse on Gibou Road welcomes visitors to watch their open evaporation process. This far north, the sap run is later, often extending well into April. Gibou Road is off Route 118 just south of town, and passes a covered bridge just after its intersection; 802-326-4775.

Montgomery has an attraction no other New England town can boast, although they go largely unnoticed: a total of **seven covered bridges**, three of which stand above dramatic gorges. On South Richford Road the Fuller

Covered Bridge crosses Black Falls Brook. The Comstock Bridge (1883) crosses the Trout River a short distance from the Black Lantern Inn and two additional covered bridges, the Longley Bridge (1863) and the Hopkins Bridge (1875), are a short drive further west on Route 118 toward Enosburg. Just under Route 118 is the Hutchins Bridge (1883), which sits astride a falls and gorge. Ask your innkeeper for a map showing the locations of all the bridges, which you can visit on a short driving tour; be prepared for unpaved, snow-covered roads.

EVENTS

December 31: **Fireworks** at Jay Peak; 802-988-2611.

Late February: Washington's Birthday celebration with **fireworks**, a magic show and **torchlight parade** at the ski area; 802-988-2611.

Easter: **Sunrise Service** at summit of Jay Peak, with free lift service for skiers and non-skiers; 802-988-2611.

SHOPPING AND CRAFTS

Montgomery Schoolhouse, in Montgomery Village, makes high quality, nearly indestructible, wooden toys. You can visit the workshop, where they have a factory store; 802-326-4272.

WHERE TO CURL UP BY THE FIRE

Phineas Swann B&B, in the center of Montgomery, is upscale and homey all at the same time. Big band music, elegant decor with a sense of humor, and an astonishing collection of autographed playbills are combined with the very personal flavor of two engaging hosts. The Inn's four guest rooms are decorated with a light-hearted country elegance, some share baths furnished with deep, claw-footed Victorian tubs, good for relaxing after a day of skiing; if you insist on a private bath, reserve early. Michael can tell you anything you ever wanted to know about the area, and Glen creates breakfasts you'll want to linger over until noon. We suggest skipping lunch and returning for their delectable afternoon tea. They will prepare elegant dinners for guests who make reservations with them in advance; don't pass up the chance; 802-326-4306.

The Inn on Trout River is next door to the Phineas Swann, in the fine antique-furnished Victorian home built at the turn of the century by the town's most successful citizen, C.T. Hall, who held the distinction of owning the first car in town, a Stanley Steamer. The down quilts, flannel sheets and feather pillows in its ten guest rooms feel good after a day outdoors. It has its own pub and a restaurant, where you can warm your toes by C.T.'s fireplace; 802-326-4391 or 800-338-7049.

The Black Lantern Inn began life in 1803 as a stagecoach inn, although it has come a long way toward luxury since then. Suites have fireplaces and whirlpools, and all rooms are furnished in antiques. Its candlelit dining room is well-regarded. The inn is located on the green in the village of Montgomery, just west of Montgomery Center; 802-326-4507 or 800-255-8661.

Inglenook Lodge is situated on a mountainside only a mile from the ski area, but offers plenty to attract non-skiers, too. The swimming pool and Jacuzzi are almost deserted during the day, and abundant lounge areas provide plenty of space. The giant circular fireplace with its sunken lounge is a favorite gathering spot for après ski; 802-988-2880 or 800-331-4346.

DINING

J.R's Restaurant and Pub is easy to spot by the greenhouse dining area that is a bit incongruent situated next to the old-fashioned buildings that surround it. But the window makes for a good place to have breakfast or lunch and absorb some sun while you watch the activity on Main Street. The chili is good and the sandwiches generous and inexpensive. The front of the restaurant has a more cafe-like atmosphere than the back, which more resembles a pub. Dinner is served until 10 p.m. from a surprisingly varied menu: red snapper with pecans, goat cheese ravioli with smoked salmon. J.R.'s serves breakfast from 6:30 a.m.; 802-326-4682.

Across the street from J.R.'s is a three-story mansard-roofed building known as **Kilgore's General Store**. In addition to serving the needs of the town as a general emporium and an informal gathering place anchored by a soda fountain and woodstove, the breakfasts and lunches are excellent. You can eat at the soda fountain or in the little cafe area overlooking the river at the back of the store; 802-326-3058.

NEW HAMPSHIRE

The White Mountains separate the far northern tip of the state from the southern half, and extend briefly into Maine on the east At their center is Mount Washington, the tallest peak in the northeast, which provides a focal point for the whole region.

Modern skiing as we know it began at Cranmore, in North Conway, and for many years it was the center of New England's ski world. Today, New Hampshire's primary ski country is still in the White Mountains, although a few notable ski areas lie to the south of these majestic peaks. As winter sports enthusiasts have gathered here over the years, the North Country, as it's known, has become the center for other winter sports as well, especially those which depend on a high annual snowfall.

Throughout the state are more than 6,000 miles of well-maintained snowmobile trails, in a corridor that links with trails in Maine, Vermont and Canada. There is no corner of the state that you cannot explore on a snowmobile, although the snowcover in the north is more dependable over a longer season. For information on snowmobiling and on snowmobile clubs, contact New Hampshire Snowmobile Association, 722 Route 3A, Suite 14, Bow, NH 03304-4010.

The New Hampshire Office of Travel and Tourism Development can be reached at 603-271-2666, or Box 856, Concord, NH 03302-0856. For a free pamphlet, call 603-386-4664 or 800-FUN-IN-NH . Skiers should contact **Ski New Hampshire**, Box 10, North Woodstock, NH 03262; 603-745-9396 or 800-88-SKI-NH.

MOUNT SUNAPEE

The peak known as Mount Sunapee stands above a lake of the same name, which is the focal point of a four-season vacation region. Nearby New London is a small college town, with the expected cultural climate this implies. Hanover, home of Dartmouth College, is a short drive away; Hanover is covered under Woodstock, Vermont, to which it is closer than Sunapee. For additional activities within easy reach, see the *Ascutney/Windsor, Vermont* area.

For more information contact the New London Area Chamber of Commerce, P.O. Box 532, New London, NH 03257; 603-526-6575.

FOR THOSE WHO SKI

With a vertical drop of 1510 feet, **Mount Sunapee** is the southernmost of New Hampshire's major ski areas. About half of its trails are geared towards intermediates. Previously operated by the state of New Hampshire, its management has recently been assumed by the people who run Okemo in Vermont, a move which skiers applaud, although locals remain doubtful. The result has been the replacement of antiquated lifts and other major improvements in the facilities; 603-763-2356.

Ragged Mountain, in Danbury, is a little-known local ski area with enough vertical drop and trails to make it attractive to non-locals. Its 32 trails are almost equally divided among all skill levels, and the mountain has almost 100% snowmaking capability. Six lifts service the mountain, and the longest trail is 1-3/4 miles. The rates make Ragged Mountain especially attractive: $30 for lift tickets on weekends, or a lesson/rental/lift package for $60; 603-768-3475, snow conditions 603-768-3971, lodging 800-400-3911.

Norsk Cross Country Center, in New London, has

50 miles of trails, most of which are tracked and groomed; 603-526-4685 or 800-426-6775.

A Unique Opportunity

The **New England Handicapped Sports Association** offers people who never thought they could ski the chance to experience the sport. It also offers active skiers a chance to share their favorite winter pastime by acting as instructors, guides and blockers, or those who warn other skiers of the approach of a blind skier. A special wheelchair-accessible lodge and a separate learning slope welcome participants to Sunapee, the association's headquarters. To become a part of this program, call 800-628-4484.

Outdoor Activities

The infrastructure of tourism is fairly low key in the Sunapee area, with few organized events or activities. The ski area, although professionally operated, is in a state-owned park, which means that it is not overdeveloped, nor are its slopes lined by trailside condos. The atmosphere is quiet, and although a lot of people here snowshoe, ski cross-country, ice fish and ride snowmobiles, they do it largely without organized help.

Norsk Cross Country Center, on Route 11 in New London, has trails for **snowshoeing** as well as skiing. Rent your snowshoes at **Village Sports**, 140 Main Street, in the center of town, where is also the place to rent **ice skates** and to find out where the best skating is at any particular time. Conditions vary with the season, and John Kiernan at Village Sports always knows which ponds and rinks are cleared and safe; 603-526-4948.

One of our favorite **snowshoe** and cross-country routes in the state is close by. A train line once connected the towns of Newport and Claremont, both just west of

Sunapee. The track and trains are gone, but the level route along the Sugar River is still there, and offers nearly ten miles of riverside trail. But it gets better: en route it passes through two rare **covered railroad bridges**. Sugar River Drive parallels the south bank of the river, and you can join the trail from any of several points along its route, since it crosses or runs alongside the road several times.

Another good place for **snowshoeing or cross-country skiing** is along the shores of Kezar Lake and through the adjoining woodlands of **Wadleigh State Park**. Begin at the village of North Sutton on Route 114, near the **Follansbee Inn** (see *Lodging*, below). Two weekends during the winter, Follansbee Inn invites guests to join their **snowshoeing weekends**. A snowshoe outfitter brings all the equipment and begins with lessons in this easy winter sport. Everyone then grabs a boxed lunch and snowshoes to a picnic site. The inn has even arranged to have a massage therapist on hand afterward to ease any muscles unused to a day's walking through the snow; 603-927-4221 or 800-626-4221.

Musterfield Farm, also in Sutton, offers some of the most interesting places to **snowshoe or cross-country ski**. This hilltop farm is now a museum, and although it is not open in the winter, it is fun to follow the trails among its barns and buildings, which include an octagonal spring house and the **ice house**. Stop to peek into this sawdust-lined building filled with big blocks of ice cut from Kezar Lake. Better yet, be on hand for the cutting, on **Ice Day**, in January (see *Events*, below).

INDOOR ACTIVITIES

Nunsuch Dairy, on Route 114 in South Sutton, is typical of the small, nearly unknown agricultural enterprises that exist all over northern New England. Courtney Haase raises Toggenburg goats, and in a spotless dairy located on the premises, she makes their milk into cheese sought by restaurants and, when there is any left over, is occasionally found in Boston specialty stores. You can visit the dairy, meet the goats, and buy soft or hard cheese at prices so low you'll think you misunderstood; 603-927-4176.

North of New London, Enfield was the site of one of New England's few **Shaker Villages**. Several of the Shaker buildings remain, including the largest Shaker Dwelling House in existence. Four-and-one-half stories tall, built of solid gray granite, the house towers over the village. Its interior has the spare simplicity that characterizes the Shaker style, and has recently been restored painstakingly to its original state to become a fine inn. The **Enfield Shaker Museum** is open Saturday from 10-4 and Sunday from 12-4 from mid-October through May, with excellent displays interpreting the Shaker way of life. Small shops at the museum and in the Inn sell fine Shaker reproductions and other Shaker-related items. You can see the beautiful stone buildings and mammoth barn and stay in the inn (see *Lodging*, below) on weekdays when the museum is closed; 603-632-4346.

Newport Opera House is an 1888 brick building, recently restored and listed on the National Register. Richly detailed, with terracotta work and stained glass, it is open weekdays and for concerts. Request a schedule; 603-863-2412.

EVENTS

Mid-January: **Ice Day** at Musterfield Farm Museum at Kezar Lake in North Sutton is an annual harvesting of ice by hand saws, using antique equipment. Old-fashioned winter pleasures fill the day: **sleigh rides, ice skating, and snowshoeing**. Homemade hot soups are served throughout the day in the 1810 schoolhouse. Watch the weather for this event, since a warm spell could thaw the ice. To be sure the event is on, call 603-927-4276 or 603-927-4646.

Mid-December: **Christmas Cookie Fair**, Enfield Shaker Village, Route 4-A in Enfield, where you can select from over 100 varieties of homemade cookies, sold by the pound. Admission is free, but go early, since the cookies don't last long; 603-632-4346.

WHERE TO CURL UP BY THE FIRE

The Shaker Inn, on Route 4-A in Enfield, serves two great causes at once: saving and restoring a one-of-a-kind historic building and providing a wonderful place to stay and to eat. Guests sleep in rooms which once housed the brothers and sisters of the Shaker community, complete with their built-in cabinetry and wall pegs. The spacious, bright rooms are furnished in fine Shaker reproductions, and one bonus of staying there is that you get a tour of the building, including its bell-tower with views of the lake and surrounding area. November packages include Thanksgiving and a weekend of cooking classes with the inn's chef, or come at Christmas, when the neighboring LaSalette Shrine is lighted for the holidays; 603-632-7810.

Freshly baked scones or muffins always highlight the breakfasts at **The Inn on Canaan Street**, in the small settlement known as Canaan Street. It's the last house on a mile of distinguished old homes that line this wide boulevard in the middle of nowhere; the inn is furnished in antiques and surely among the quietest of all B&Bs; 603-523-7310.

The Inn at Pleasant Lake, on Pleasant Street in New London, has 11 attractive rooms with either woodland views or a sweeping vista across the lake to Mount Kearsarge. Two rooms have whirlpool baths. Arrive early enough for afternoon tea with fresh-baked sweets; 603-526-6271 or 800-626-4907.

Riverview Farms Inn, five minutes from New London in the village of Wilmot Flat, is the best of both worlds. It has the congenial warmth of a B&B, but you don't have to make—or listen to—breakfast conversation. Each two-room suite has its own coffee maker, microwave and refrigerator (stocked with wine and cheese), and the innkeeper brings muffins and breakfast pastries the night before, so you can begin your day on your own schedule. Marie, the lively innkeeper, is a goldmine of information on what to do and see in the local area and provides guests with maps and information guides; 603-526-4482 or 800-392-9627.

Follansbee Inn, overlooking Kezar Lake in North Sutton, is an old-fashioned—but not frumpy—inn where families return for generations. In the winter, fireplaces make it a cozy, welcoming place to come home to after skiing or snowshoeing on Wadleigh State Park's trails, just a brief ski away. Guest rooms are bright, some with handmade vintage quilts, and a full breakfast begins each day; 603-927-4221 or 800-626-4221.

DINING

Sweet Tomatoes, in the center of nearby Lebanon, is one of the area's outstanding restaurants, with top quality fresh ingredients prepared in a giant wood-fired oven. Pizzas are only the beginning of the dishes they offer, all filled with the earthy rich flavors of grilled vegetables, fine olive oil and fresh herbs. Service is upbeat and the atmosphere lively; 603-448-1711.

The Shaker Inn, in Enfield, serves creative and more conventional dishes, some of which are based on Shaker ingredients, especially the variety of herbs grown in the museum's restored gardens. An historian and herb gardener from the museum prepares background notes on the Shakers and their cooking to accompany each menu. But you don't have to be remotely interested in the history to enjoy the excellent entrees here: rack of lamb with maple-balsamic glaze, duck sauced in rhubarb and ginger, or perfectly cooked salmon crusted in horseradish. The desserts are far too sinful to be served in a place where such righteous people once lived; 603-632-7810.

Cliff Lodge, at the southern shore of Newfound Lake above Route 3A just north of Bristol, is only ten minutes from Ragged Mountain, about 35 minutes from New London. The cozy dining room overlooks the sunset, but we go for the food, an inspired blend of New American and Cuban in the hands of a French-born chef. It's the best of all these on one plate. The regular menu has a wide range of choices, each with some tantalizing out-of-the-ordinary difference that makes us want to order it. But the specials go all out: saddle of lamb *en croute* or swordfish that melts in your mouth, crisply coated in sesame seeds and fresh grated ginger, and served with a blend of plantain and chorizo...well, you get the idea. Patrice has a real way with fish, and lets the flavors of fresh vegetables shine through. Prices are moderate, and much less than such outstanding fare costs elsewhere. Open in winter Thursday through Monday from 5-9 p.m., closed April; 603-744-8660.

Also well-prepared, elegant and beautifully presented, although with limited choices, are candlelit dinners at **The Inn at Pleasant Lake**, on Pleasant Street in New London. Dining here is a unique experience, with guests gathering first for a brief preview of the evening's menu, presented by the amiable chef-owner. The menu is fixed, as is the price, with a choice of a fish or meat entree each evening. Each of the five courses receives the chef's full attention, with tiny details such as a drizzle of chive-infused oil over the potato-onion cream soup or the chef's own red grape dressing on the salad of mixed spring greens. Dinner is at 7 p.m., by reservation, on Tuesday through Sunday in the winter; 603-526-6271 or 800-626-4907.

Murphy's Grille, on Route 103 at the Mount Sunapee Traffic Circle in Sunapee, is a family-friendly grill serving lunch and dinner daily and weekend breakfasts. All the usual suspects—steaks, grilled chicken, fajitas, sandwiches, pasta, burgers—are generously served and moderately priced; 603-763-3113.

GUNSTOCK AND THE LAKES REGION

T he Lakes Region became the site of America's first summer cottage when Royal Governor John Wentworth built a house in Wolfeboro. Visitors have been coming ever since to enjoy the scenic contrasts of the Belknap Range and the many lakes that lie at its feet. Laconia is the largest city; Wolfeboro, Meredith and Center Harbor also front onto Lake Winnipesaukee.

Wolfeboro is a nice town at any season, with views over Lake Winnipesaukee (you have to have grown up here to spell that without checking) and some pleasant Main Street eateries; we enjoy the informal atmosphere—and the homemade pies—at Mast Landing, right in the center of town.

For information on the Lakes Region, contact the Greater Laconia/Weirs Beach Chamber of Commerce, 11 Veteran's Square, Laconia, NH 03246; 603-524-5531 or 800-531-2347. Or contact The Lakes Region Association, Center Harbor, NH 03226; 603-253-8555 or 800-60-LAKES. Wolfeboro Chamber of Commerce, 32 Central Avenue, Wolfeboro, NH 03894; 603-569-2200 or 800-516-5324.

FOR THOSE WHO SKI

Gunstock, in Gilford, offers skiers 45 trails on a vertical drop of 1400 feet. More than half the trails are intermediate, but 11 are classed as expert; 603-293-4341 or 800-GUNSTOCK.

Gunstock Cross Country Ski Center is located at the downhill area, and offers about 30 miles of trails with warming huts; 603-293-4341 or 800-GUNSTOCK. **Nordic Center** in Wolfeboro is smaller, with about 12 miles of trails; 603-569-3151. Both offer night skiing. **Red Hill**

Inn's Ski Touring Center, although it has only three miles of trails, has one advantage not many others offer: it's free. Equipment rental is available; 603-279-7001.

OUTDOOR ACTIVITIES

The **Science Center of New Hampshire**, on Squam Lake (Route 113) in Holderness, has a full calendar of nature activities year round. Winter programs include **animal tracking, bird-banding, small-scale maple sugaring, snowshoe hikes and winter sky stargazing** evenings. During the latter you will learn to identify specific constellations, planets and stars and learn to read star charts. Costs vary, but the bird-banding morning and the stargazing class cost only $3; members are free. You do need reservations for most events; 603-968-7194.

INDOOR ACTIVITIES

Wright Museum divides its space and energy between the Home Front and the military, so it is interesting even to those who don't know a tank from a torpedo. Along with showcase displays of everything from ration books to big bands, are a full kitchen and living room from the war era, and a soda fountain. The military building features an excellent presentation on the WASPS, the women's branch of the Army Air Corps, with filmed interviews in which these women look back at their experiences, interspersed with live footage of their bases and work during the war. Military vehicles fill the center of the building and displays are on both levels of the gallery around them. These include the experiences of a local serviceman, front pages of the Honolulu newspapers the morning after Pearl Harbor, and a collection of "nose art" from fighter planes based on Saipan. For its variety and the rather good job they've done with mounting displays, it's an interesting place to go. 77

Center Street (Routes 109 and 28), close to the marina; 603-569-1212. Winter hours are 10 a.m. to 4 p.m., Saturday and Sunday. Admission is charged, with student, senior and veteran discounts.

In the center of Laconia, **The Belknap Mill** is the oldest unaltered brick textile mill in America. It contains a museum of the textile industry—with working machines—the region's arts and entertainment center; 603-524-8813.

All winter, on the first and third Fridays of each month, the Wolfeboro Wranglers have held **square dances** for the past several years at 8 p.m. at the Middle School. They may not continue, so you'd better call first Admission is $3.50 and lessons are available; 603-569-2885.

Operating between Tilton and Laconia, **Dinner Train** coaches are equipped with special lighting to illuminate the scenery as it passes. Departures from either station are at 6 p.m. on weekend evenings, except for the special Santa Trains, which run during the day. Reservations are a must; 603-745-2135.

EVENTS

Early December: Center Sandwich, a town long known for its fine crafts tradition, holds a **Craftsmen's Open House**, with open studios and the Town Hall filled with crafts. Demonstrations include weaving and spinning. A horse and buggy will take visitors for rides around the scenic village. Admission is free; 603-284-6915.

New Years Eve: A **First Night** celebration rings in the New Year in Wolfeboro with music, singing, fireworks and other entertainment; 603-569-2200.

Mid-January: Gunstock's annual **Snowfest Weekend** includes wagon rides and live entertainment, in addition to ski-related events; 603-293-4341 or 800-GUNSTOCK.

Mid-February: The Annual Great Rotary Fishing Derby brings **ice fishing** enthusiasts from all over, who may enter fish caught elsewhere in the state; 603-569-2200 or 800-516-5324.

SHOPPING AND CRAFTS

Keepsake Quilting, which bills itself as America's largest quilt shops (we've always wondered exactly how they arrive at these figures) is filled with nearly 6,000 bolts of quilting fabrics and every tool imaginable for the craft, as well as finished quilts. It's in Senter's Marketplace in Center Harbor; 800-865-9458.

Pepi Herman Crystal Studio, near the Laconia airport in Guilford, offers tours of its museum and the studio where crystal is hand-cut. They are open Tuesday through Saturday; 603-528-1020 or 800-HANDCUT.

WHERE TO CURL UP BY THE FIRE

Red Hill Inn began life as a private mansion over a century ago, and has been restored to its original interior, with some important comforts added. The woodwork is beautiful. Hospitality is warm and the dining room is memorable. Their small cross-country ski center has rental equipment and *no* trail fees; 603-279-7001 or 800-5-REDHILL.

The Nutmeg Inn in Meredith was built in 1763, and retains many of its antique features, including wide boards and secret passages. Some rooms have fireplaces, all have the individuality that makes historic places interesting; 603-279-8811.

The Margate at Winnipesaukee is a full-service resort with well-furnished rooms and a spa with indoor pool, sauna, whirlpool and exercise room; 603-524-5210 or 800-627-4283.

DINING

Bittersweet, south of Wolfeboro, offers an interesting menu with influences from all over—wienerschnitzel,

Italian specialties, and unusual offerings such as lamb and cider pie. The decor is informal, with country antiques; 603-569-3636.

Victorian House, on Route 11 in Gilford, is in an 1821 stagecoach inn, its fine Victorian architectural features restored and embellished by a skillful decorator with a sense of humor. But it's not the decor you're interested in, it's the menu. Changing seasonally, it pairs fine New England-raised meats and produce with a whole world of seasonings and cooking styles. We don't usually eat desserts, but couldn't resist the nut torte here. Open Tuesday through Sunday for dinner only; 603-293-8155

The Cider Press in Wolfeboro serves all the favorites—steaks, chops, chicken, fresh seafood—in a country decor highlighted by a large fireplace in the dining room; 603-569-2028.

WATERVILLE VALLEY AND LOON MOUNTAIN

Waterville Valley is unusual in New Hampshire in that it is the only cul-de-sac, self-contained ski resort in the state. This insulated security makes it especially attractive to families, since children can ride a free valley shuttle bus from the slopes to their lodgings, or to the skating rink or any other of the many valley activities. It makes Waterville a good choice for families with both skiers and non-skiers, too, since you don't need a car to get to the slopes or to the other activities. Special programs are offered on and off slopes for teens. It is one of the easiest areas to reach for those arriving from southern New England, since it lies close to I-93.

Also close to the Interstate is Loon Mountain, which has awakened the town of Lincoln from its post-lumber-boom doldrums, making it a vibrant community again. Close to—or at—the slopes are dining, lodging, entertainment and a host of activities. Both Loon and Waterville have a heavy family clientele.

For more information on the region, contact the Lincoln/Woodstock Chamber of Commerce, Lincoln, NH 03251; 603-745-6621. The White Mountain Attractions Association covers attractions throughout the entire northern part of the state. Stop by their headquarters at the intersection of Route 112 (the Kancamagus Highway) and I-93 in Lincoln, or write to them at P.O. Box 10, North Woodstock, NH 03262; 603-745-8720 or 800-FIND-MTS.

FOR THOSE WHO SKI

The family orientation of **Waterville Valley** means that the variety of trails for novice and intermediate skiers are greater than at some other areas, with ten novice and 38 intermediate trails. But the top of the mountain has a sheer face, so its ten remaining trails offer considerable challenge. It has the largest lift capacity of any New Hampshire area, an award-winning ski school for children and an adaptive skiing program for mentally or physically challenged adults and children. To reach Waterville, take Route 49 east from I-93 at Campton; 603-236-8311 or 800-GO-VALLEY.

Loon Mountain has the second greatest vertical drop in the state, at 3100 feet. Two high-speed detachable quads speed skiers up its precipitous face, which is traversed by 43 trails—27 of which are classed as intermediate—and acres of glades. It is one of the most modern ski facilities in New England, with an excellent range of slopeside facilities. Grooming these north-facing trails is a real challenge, so be prepared for icy conditions. Skiers can transfer between base lodges on a former logging train engine, which wheezes and puffs along a short section of track; 603-745-8111.

Cross-country skiers will find about 20 miles of trails at **Loon Mountain** and 60 at **Waterville**. In nearby Thornton, **Sugar Shack Nordic Village** has about 20 miles of trails and adds night skiing to its attractions; 603-726-3867. All three have warming huts.

INDOOR ACTIVITIES

The **Wildlife Theater** at Loon Mountain isn't just for kids. Daily shows featuring native and exotic birds and animals are just as fascinating to adults. While watching the creatures, which usually include snakes, ferrets and a baby mountain lion, participants learn about their habits and the efforts that people are making to protect their habitat and the environment they live in; the chance to pet a snake is irresistible. Children under 5 are admitted free; 603-745-6281, ext. 5538.

Loon's **Children's Theater** presents skilled storytellers re-creating folk stories and fairy tales in a setting that encourages listeners to become part of the story. The cast of four sings, dances, and acts out light-hearted stories that delight children and bring a smile to parents' faces. Performances are on weekends and during vacation weeks at the Octagon Lodge; 603-745-6281, ext. 5538.

Waterville's **White Mountain Athletic Club** has tennis, squash and racquetball courts, a 75-foot indoor swimming pool, jogging track, equipment room, saunas, whirlpools, steam rooms, and game room, most of which are blissfully uncrowded during the day; 603-236-8311.

The same is true at **The Fitness Center** at Loon's Mountain Club, whose amenities include an indoor pool and outdoor whirlpool, exercise equipment, and racquet courts. Show a lift ticket for the same day and get a 50% discount; 603-745-2244, ext. 5280.

OUTDOOR ACTIVITIES

Loon's **skating rink** is lighted at night, with rental skates available at the Cross Country Center's rental shop.

Ice skating is indoors at **Waterville Valley**, on a well-manicured rink inside a refrigerated arena. You can skate on Zamboni-groomed ice from October through April, even when it's sloshy outside. A warming area and rental/repair shop are part of the rink. The arena is open for public skating mornings, afternoons and evenings, and lessons are available. If you don't want to skate, you can watch the hockey games; call ahead for the hockey schedule and for public skating times; 603-236-4813.

Sleigh rides on The Waterville Valley Flier, a big wagon-style double sled pulled by a team of Percherons, circle the valley floor for views of the surrounding mountains. A smaller single sleigh is pulled by a single horse. They leave from Town Square both afternoons and evenings. Bring an apple or carrot to feed the Percherons; they're very gentle-mannered and will eat right out of your hand. You should make reservations for sleigh rides; 603-

236-8311, ext. 300.

Horseback riding is a year-round sport at Waterville. Saddle horses are available at the stables, near the base of Snow's Mountain; 603-236-8311, ext. 300.

Waterville Valley's **Base Camp** conducts **snowshoe tours** for people of all skill levels, including one for intermediates on Boulder Trail. The route passes a giant glacial erratic, a boulder dropped by the retreating glacier at the close of the Ice Age. The views of the valley are superb on another tour for intermediates known as the Sloppy Joe Tour which involves some uneven terrain and a short climb. All the tours are led by people well-versed in the local wildlife, history, geology and in the techniques of snowshoeing, so you learn a lot as well as have fun. You can rent Tubbs snowshoes at the Base Camp, or buy a pair at the shop there; 603-236-4666.

Snowshoes may also be rented at Loon Mountain's Cross Country Center, and First Ascent Climbing School offers guided snowshoe tours as well as renting the equipment; 603-745-2867. Loon also has a **tubing park**, open evenings from 5:30-10 p.m., with a 2600-foot trail and tubes for rent at the West Basin rental shop.

S&J Snowmobile Rentals, on Lost River Road in North Woodstock (about two miles from Loon Mountain), rents machines on weekdays only. On weekends, they only rent them only in conjunction with their guided tours. Even during the week, you must spend the first hour of your rental with a guide, who will make sure you know the machine and the local conditions before you go out on your own. Guided tours in the National Forest are on groomed trails, with guides who know the trails well. Three-hour twilight tours take riders along the shores of Bog Pond to a campfire in the snow. They also rent appropriate clothing and provide helmets free of charge; 603-745-6123.

CHRISTMAS EVENTS

The two weekends prior to Christmas: **Northern Lights**

in Town Square at Waterville includes caroling for all and the arrival of Santa Claus, who will stay for photos.

Christmas Day: A two-hour **Dinner Train Ride** leaves Lincoln at 6 p.m. for a ride through the snow-covered valley and a five-course dinner; reservations are essential; 603-745-3500.

EVENTS

Late December: **Hobo Railroad**, in Lincoln, has afternoon train rides each day between Christmas and New Years Eve. Trains leave Lincoln at 2 p.m., with cookies and hot cocoa available on board; 603-745-2135.

New Year's Eve: Waterville Valley celebrates with a **torchlight parade** and skiing; 603-236-4666.

Mid-February: **Waterville Winter Carnival** includes a torchlight parade through the valley by cross-country skiers, a snow sculpture contest, family broomball, a bonfire, skating with cartoon characters, and sled dog races. The latter are held to benefit a camp for terminally ill children. To get involved, call Mary Ann Rossi at Waterville Valley Shirt Company; 603-236-4660. For information about Winter Carnival activities, call 603-236-8311.

Early March: End of the season **Ice Show** at the Ice Arena, Waterville Valley; 603-236-4813.

Late March: Waterville's **Sam Adams Micro-Brew Fest and Cookout**, held slopeside at Murphy's BBQ, with nine New England breweries participating.

Easter: **Sunrise Services** are held at the summits of Mount Tecumseh at Waterville and of Loon Mountain.

Easter: The Annual **Easter Egg Hunt** is at noon at the Millfront Marketplace in Lincoln; 603-745-2245.

SHOPPING AND CRAFTS

Town Square, at Waterville Valley, is a compact area of shops at the base of the mountain. You'll find food at

Jugtown Deli, clothing, gifts and husky-related items at **Waterville Valley Shirt Company**, books at **The Bookmonger,** and gifts at **Daphne's**. The shops encircle an open plaza where resort activities and entertainments are frequently held.

The Mill at Loon Mountain contains shops, restaurants, movies and entertainment in the center of Lincoln. For a good selection of books on the White Mountains and New Hampshire in general, visit **Innisfree Bookshop** in the Millfront Shops; 603-745-6107.

A Special Christmas Package

Waterville Valley has a real bargain in store for families who choose to spend Christmas there: a four-day package with all the frills runs about $700 for a family of four. The deal includes lodging, lift tickets, a sleigh ride, skating party and snow-cat ride, and other goodies. Use of the sports facilities is included, too; 800-GO-VALLEY.

Where To Curl Up By The Fire

The Snowy Owl is the perfect combination of luxury inn and ski lodge, with the comfort and facilities of one and the camaraderie of the other. A huge fieldstone fireplace dominates the first floor lobby, and an equally large one directly below it is sunken with benches forming a mini amphitheater around it. Everyone gathers around these in the late afternoon for wine and cheese and again in the evening for games, singing and conversation. We like the double-decker rooms with kid's bunks in the lofts and giant Jacuzzis. Warm wood tones and alpine-feel furnishings set a nice tone. The large indoor heated pool is popular with everyone; 603-236-8371 or 800-GO-VALLEY.

Golden Eagle Lodge is a full-service resort hotel, with a two-story fireplace, large lobby, and nicely appointed suites with full kitchens. It has an indoor pool with saunas and, whirlpools and a game room; 603-236-8371 or 800-GO-VALLEY.

The Valley Inn is a well-run hotel with some resort facilities of its own, but guests have free access to all Waterville Valley sports facilities as well. Rooms range from spacious, elegant suites with whirlpool baths and full kitchens, to smaller, comfortable and very budget-minded rooms on the lower floor near the indoor/outdoor pool. These run as low as $59 in midwinter, including breakfast. We applaud this diversity, as well as the most accommodating staff. Nice decorative touches, including solid cherry woodwork and hand painted hallways, have recently added to the hotel's high quality atmosphere. We make our reservations in the dining room when we reserve our room here; 603-236-8366 or 800-GO-VALLEY.

Black Bear Lodge is a comfortable, hospitable condo-style lodge with economical suites for four to six people. An indoor/outdoor pool, sauna, steam room, game room and exercise room are on the premises; 603-236-8383 or 800-GO-VALLEY.

The Mill House Inn is a modern hotel on Route 112 in Lincoln that's close to Loon Mountain. It features an indoor pool, Jacuzzis and saunas, exercise room, tennis courts, and an enclosed walkway to shops, restaurants and entertainment in the adjacent shopping complex. A free shuttle carries guests to Loon Mountain; 603-745-6261 or 800-654-6183.

The Mountain Club on Loon is in the center of the slopeside recreation park and convenient to everything. Condo-style rooms are well furnished and roomy, and the lodge has abundant public areas, including two pools, game rooms, ball courts, and a fully equipped fitness center. The staff is efficient and exceedingly accommodating in this well-managed resort; 603-745-3441 or 800-229-STAY.

Mountain-Fare Inn, on Mad River Road in Campton, is an old-fashioned ski lodge and inn, with antique furnishings, fireplaces and hearty breakfasts. It has ten rooms and suites, moderately priced; 603-726-4283.

Wilderness Inn B&B is set in a 1912 country estate at Routes 3 and 112 in North Woodstock. Afternoon tea is served by the fireside and full breakfasts are sumptuous. Seven bedrooms, plus a family suites and a cottage are all reasonably priced, especially for such a fine setting; 603-745-3890 or 800-200-WILD.

DINING

IN THE WATERVILLE VALLEY AREA:

Chile Peppers, at Waterville Town Square, serves all the old Tex Mex favorites—enchiladas, fajitas, nachos, guacamole, quesadillas—plus barbecued and grilled meats, in a casual south-of-the-border atmosphere; 603-236-4646.

The Common Man, also at Waterville Town Square, is a branch of the popular Ashland restaurant, serving American food in hearty portions. They also have a bar menu of lighter dishes; 603-236-8885.

Coffee Emporium, upstairs over Chile Peppers, serves waffles, omelets and other breakfast and brunch dishes as well as sandwiches and sinfully good cakes and tortes in an upbeat cafe atmosphere.

We haven't eaten at the **Wild Coyote Grill** in the White Mountain Athletic Club, but we've heard good things about it, and from chefs we admire. The menu may include fresh mussels, walnut encrusted pork chops, Caesar salad with grilled shrimp, marinated slow roasted chicken and a five-onion soup; 603-236-4919.

The Valley Inn has, for our money, the most memorable dining room in the Valley complex, serving interesting entrees created by a very talented chef. The setting is the most elegant at the ski area; 603-236-8366.

Schwendi Hutte, at the summit of Mount Tecumseh, serves hearty alpine lunches and outdoor barbecues on the sundeck when the winter temperatures permit. Possibly the most romantic dining experience in the Valley is on Saturday evenings, when a three-course dinner is served after a ride to the top of the mountain by snow-cat. You do need to reserve; 603-236-8311.

It's a close finish in the romance race between Schwendi Hutte and the trip to Switzerland offered at **The William Tell** on Route 49 toward Campton. Small tables, an intimate atmosphere and just the right amount of Swiss decor (it's so easy to overdo this theme, and they don't) make this a dining experience, not just a fine dinner. The veal is always superb, and whatever you order, ask for *rosti*, a crisp potato dish, to go with it. Theirs is better than most we've had in Switzerland. We haven't tried their fondue, but friends rave about it; 603-726-3618.

IN THE LINCOLN/LOON AREA:

The Common Man, a third location of this local restaurant, located at the corner of Pollard Road and the Kancamagus Highway; 603-745-DINE.

The Woodstock Inn, in the center of North Woodstock, has a dining room and the more casual **Woodstock Station**, with a brewpub serving up the product of Woodstock Brewing Company; 603-745-3951.

Frannie's, on Route 3, half a mile south of I-93's Exit 30 in Thornton, hides a good menu behind a plain exterior. Long a favorite of snowmobilers, this family-friendly restaurant offers plentiful portions of well-prepared and often imaginative dishes. Don't miss the coleslaw; 603-745-3868.

CRANMORE, ATTITASH AND THE MOUNT WASHINGTON VALLEY

Northconway in the winter is a classic ski town. The town boomed in the early days of the sport, when the Ski Train brought carloads of people from New York and Boston each Friday evening. New times and pleasures have changed the town the rest of the year, but there's still some of that old excitement here in the winter. As New Hampshire's major outlet shopping center, North Conway is busy year-round. Its après ski crowd blends—sometimes oddly—with the après spend crowd. The visual and geographical center of the town is the grand and beautiful railway station, the same one that welcomed the Ski Trains.

For information on the area, contact The Mount Washington Valley Chamber of Commerce, P.O. Box 2300, North Conway, NH 03860; 603-356-3171 or 800-367-3364 for reservations. The White Mountain Attractions Association covers attractions throughout the entire northern part of the state. Contact them at P.O. Box 10, North Woodstock, NH 03262; 603-745-8720 or 800-FIND-MTS.

FOR THOSE WHO SKI

Cranmore was the very first ski area in America, founded by the legendary Hannes Schneider, known as the father of modern skiing. Since the 1930s, Cranmore has attracted skiers of all skills, first with its Skimobile ride up the mountain, now with a high-speed superquad lift and five others. Night skiing, 100% snowmaking and panoramic views over the mountains and valley add to its sunny southwest exposure to keep it a popular area for all kinds of skiers. For information call 603-356-5543 or 800-SUN-N-SKI.

Attitash/Bear Peak is one of New England's newer ski areas, and its approach to skiing is always innovative, whether it's in creating a "Perfect Turn Clinic," free guided demos of the latest super sidecut skis or a pay-by-the-run ski ticket. Trails and lifts connect two peaks, one of which has a novice trail from the top. It's on Route 302 in Bartlett, north of North Conway; 800-223-SNOW.

Also within easy reach are Black Mountain and Wildcat; see *Jackson*.

Cross-country skiers can choose from the most trails of any area in the east, all within easy reach of North Conway. **Bear Notch Ski Touring Center**, in Bartlett, not far from Attitash, has 60 miles of trails, with exceptionally low trail fees and a **moonlight ski** every month skiing. Fees are $6 weekdays, $10 on weekends and holidays (ages under 12 and over 70 free); 603-374-2277. **Mount Washington Valley Ski Touring**, in Intervale (just north of North Conway), has 35 miles of trails with warming huts; 603-356-9920.

OUTDOOR ACTIVITIES

Joe Jones and the Appalachian Mountain Club (see *Pinkham Notch*) rent **snowshoes**. You can follow old woods roads or create your own trails almost anywhere. **Great Glen Trails** has snowshoe trails. To buy **custom snowshoes**, go to Baldy's on the Kancamagus Highway approach road out of Conway. Trefflee Bolduc learned his snowshoe-making skills from French Canadian and Indian craftsmen; 603-447-5287.

Whenever the temperatures drop below freezing, **skating** is popular on the public rink in North Conway right in front of train station. In nearby Jackson, **Nestlenook Farm** has skating on its pond, decorated in a Victorian theme; see *Jackson*.

To learn **ice climbing** on some of the best terrain around—Cathedral and White Horse Ledges—contact International Mountain Equipment in North Conway. Rick

Wilcox is a well-recognized expert, and a veteran of Mount Everest expeditions; 603-356-7064.

SHOPPING AND CRAFTS

In North Conway, when evening talk around the fireplace turns to the length of the lines that day, people are talking about checkout lines, not lift lines. Even at the height of ski season, on any day there will be more shoppers in the outlets than skiers on the surrounding slopes.

For some, the abundance of outlets here is overwhelming. Everywhere you look are outlets, in malls, in little clusters that don't quite make it to mall status, by themselves along Route 16, even retrofitted into little cottages by the wayside. Whatever it is you hope to find at outlet prices, it's bound to be here. Along with so many other things you didn't know you wanted, the experience is likely to be more expensive than if you'd just gone to your local department store. But that is hardly a sporting attitude; the game is shopping and this is Yankee Stadium.

Before you sharpen the edges of your Visa card for a weekend on the bargain trails, it may help to have a short refresher course in Shopping 101. Remember that all outlets are not created equal. Some are no more than company-run stores where goods sell at close to list prices, with occasional sales like any other store. Others are genuine factory outlets, with overruns, seconds, returns from catalog sales, and a general assortment of leftovers at significant savings. To know the difference, it's wise to know the price of items you're looking for before you hit the outlets. The stores to look for are those you don't see in every outlet mall, those one-or-two-of-a-kind places where the manufacturer sends the tired, the poor, the huddled masses of men's shirts that have already been tried on— we've always thought it was a blessing to have someone else take out all those cursed little pins—last year's trendy colors, and woolens in mid-June.

Before you hit the malls, check into your lodgings first,

since most motels and inns near the malls include a booklet of coupons in your check-in packet. These can provide you with a further discount or entitle you to a free gift with purchase. After all, if you're there for the bargains, why not get them all? Settlers Green, Tanger Factory Outlet Center, and L.L. Bean Center are the largest of the complexes.

For a refreshing non-outlet experience, and a chance to find really nice New England-made products from food to crafts, go to **Zeb's General Store**, on Main Street, opposite the Railway Station; 603-356-9294.

And for bargains from a real live home-grown company, visit **Chuck Roast Mountainwear**, on Route 16. Their rugged, warm, well-styled outdoor gear is guaranteed for life *period*, no matter how often or hard you use it. Bargains at their store include discounts of 10-60% on vests, jackets, mittens, hats, packs, children's clothing and more; 603-356-5589.

INDOOR ACTIVITIES

For visitors who don't enjoy shopping, North Conway is still attractive for its lively atmosphere and fine scenery, and in certain circles it's very chic to be just a little disdainful of the shopping.

The Bernerhof Inn and Prince's Place Restaurant in Glen offers "A Taste of the Mountains," a unique **cooking school** in their Victorian mansion. Weekend and weeklong programs are offered for serious cooks and novices, with lodging, classes and all meals included. Every Thursday, a three-hour hands-on class is given by a different guest chef, after which participants enjoy a memorable meal; 603-383-4414 or 800-548-8007.

EVENTS

Thanksgiving Weekend: The **Conway Scenic Railroad** offers late-season rides in heated cars, which leave the

North Conway station in the afternoon; 603-356-5251.

December: **The Polar Express** makes eight memorable runs from the station in North Conway to The North Pole, where kids of all ages find a magical world. Based on the popular children's book by Chris Van Allsburg, it's the story of a little boy who refuses to join his friends who scoff at Santa Claus. But as he lies awake on Christmas Eve he hears not sleighbells, but the hissing of a steam locomotive. A conductor invites him to join in the trip to the North Pole, and it is that magical trip that the Conway Scenic Railroad so lovingly re-creates. The attention to detail is superb: wolves prowl the woods, and elves populate the North Pole. Many passengers join in the spirit of the trip by boarding in pajamas and robes. Tickets, at $18 for adults and $12 for children, go on sale October 21, and don't last very long. Passengers over age 90 ride free, but will still need to reserve a space; 800-337-3563.

December: **Wintry Trails Decorating Contest** adds even more sparkle to the snowy landscape throughout the Mount Washington Valley, as homes and businesses prepare for the holidays.

December 31: Mount Washington Valley **First Night** (603-356-5701, ext. 350), culminates in a torchlight parade and fireworks at Mount Cranmore; 603-356-5543.

Late February: The **Mount Washington Valley Chocolate Festival** involves chocolate related events throughout the area, highlighted by an inn-to-inn cross country ski tour with chocolate treats at each stop; 800-367-3364.

Where To Curl Up By The Fire

Snow Village Inn, perched on a hillside, is surrounded by woods on three sides and a sweeping view of the entire skyline of the Presidential Range on the fourth. The inn tempts you to settle in for the weekend by serving sumptuous **candlelit dinners**; they serve non-guests by reservation. If you don't enjoy **snowshoeing or cross-**

country skiing on the trails that leave from the door, there's absolutely no reason to go outside. They even furnish the good books. Rooms are furnished in antiques and beds with comforters. The inn is twelve miles south of North Conway in Snowville—yes, that is really the town's name; 603-447-2818.

On Route 16A, which parallels busy Route 16 between North Conway and Glen, **The Forest Inn** is convenient to both North Conway and Jackson, but at a peaceful distanced from both. Antique furnishings are comfortable and the elegance is informal enough to relax in. We especially like the third-floor rooms set into the Mansard roof with slightly sloping walls, but all rooms are spacious and very nicely decorated. Breakfasts are bountiful and delicious; 603-356-9772 or 800-448-3534.

Farm by the River B&B, on West Side Road in North Conway, is just what it says. The 1780s farmhouse sits on 65 acres of flat river valley farmland, where you can go for a sleigh ride and enjoy views of the mountains that surround it. Breakfast is served by the fireplace; it's far too cozy to leave; 603-356-2694.

The Notchland Inn has character. The 1840 mansion of solid gray granite has fine architectural details, including its interior woodwork, and the old schoolhouse behind it—now housing beautiful guestrooms—has enough wonderful stories to fill a book. Woodburning fireplaces in all the guestrooms, Victorian period furnishings, and a very good restaurant make it even more attractive; 603-374-6131 or 800-866-6131.

The Bernerhof is an elegant inn in a Victorian mansion. Rooms are furnished in antiques and have double spa tubs. They are well known for their restaurant, which serves European specialties. They also offer cooking classes (see *above*); 603-383-4414 or 800-548-8007.

Green Granite Inn, although motel-like in its layout, bears no further resemblance to a motel. Walls of the inviting tartan-carpeted lobby are decorated with a mini-museum of stuffed wild animals, most natives to New Hampshire. Après ski wine and cheese are served here to guests, who gather in the comfortable leather couches in front of the fireplace. During winter school vacation weeks and on Saturdays, the Inn offers daylong children's programs with games, crafts and other activities, and the new solarium-enclosed indoor pool has extended hours for those who enjoy a swim before breakfast or late in the evening. Rooms are individually decorated—mostly in cherry—many have whirlpool tubs, and all gleam with the well-cared-for look of a family-run hotel. Suites and condo units sleep six or eight; some have full kitchens; 603-356-6901 or 800-468-3666.

Right in the Settlers Green outlet center is **Four Points Hotel by Sheraton**, a modern full-service hotel with all the details of a city hotel: pool, exercise room, a lighted skating rink, tennis courts, a game room, and on-site restaurants, where kids eat for 99 cents. All this and a friendly staff, too; 603-356-9300 or 800-648-4397.

DINING

New England Inn in Intervale, just north of North Conway, has a traditional Yankee menu, and a traditional New England inn setting. Look for some nice touches, like a cranberry pot roast; 603-356-5541.

Bellini's, on Seavy Street, is an intimate Italian restaurant where everything is made in-house. Fresh produce is the key to their sauces. These are so good that people buy it by the bottle to take home; 603-356-7000.

The Ledges, in the White Mountain Hotel, is best known for its Friday evening seafood buffet, but off-the-menu dinners are excellent, as is the wine list; 603-356-7100.

A bit of a distance south in West Ossipee, but nice to know about if you're out for a drive on Route 16, **Yankee Smokehouse**, which serves pork and beef ribs, roast pork, and baby back ribs cooked in their smokehouse barbecue. Bountiful portions and low prices keep them busy. Open in the winter from Thursday through Sunday; 603-539-7427.

Prince's Place, at the Bernerhof on Route 302 in Glen, balances two cuisines: classic middle European favorites including wienerschnitzel and other veal dishes, and an innovative New American menu of creative originals. Both are expertly done; 603-383-4414.

JACKSON AND PINKHAM NOTCH

The only way to get to the village of Jackson is through a red-painted covered bridge, and the center of the village is just as picturesque as its entrance. Once home to a number of grand old resort hotels, Jackson has always been popular with travelers. It is equidistant to two ski areas—and close enough to two more—that it has become the winter sports center of the eastern White Mountains.

For more information on the Jackson area, contact the Jackson Chamber of Commerce, P.O. Box 304, Jackson, NH 03846; 603-383-9356 or 800-866-3334. The White Mountain Attractions Association covers attractions throughout the entire northern part of the state. Contact them at P.O. Box 10, North Woodstock, NH 03262; 603-745-8720 or 800-FIND-MTS.

FOR THOSE WHO SKI

Black Mountain is a low-key family-friendly area, where the first pull-lift (as opposed to a rope tow which you grab onto) was invented at the adjacent Whitney's Inn. They used shovel handles, which the Whitneys ordered from Sears Roebuck. "Ma" Whitney, loved by generations of skiers, still lives on the hill overlooking the slope where they built this first T-bar prototype; 603-383-4490 or 800-475-4669.

Wildcat, north on Route 302 in Pinkham Notch, is a challenging area with a 2100-foot vertical drop, almost 200 inches of natural snowfall and the finest views in the mountains. From the top, if you dare to open your eyes once you've seen the pitch of the trails to the bottom, you look directly onto Tuckerman's Ravine and the upper reaches of Mount Washington. Some of our most terrifying moments on skis have occurred here, but we could still appreciate the view before we plunged headlong into certain death. Their motto is "Earn Bragging Rights" for good reason; 603-466-3326 or 800-255-6439.

Jackson Ski Touring has some of the finest cross-country ski trails in America, some 150 km (93 miles) of them. The trails cover the valley floor, and climb into the woods and along the ridges and hillsides that enclose Jackson. They also connect inns and restaurants so you can even plan a vacation skiing inn-to-inn. The Touring Center in the village has trail maps, ski rentals and lessons; 603-383-9355 or 800-XC-SNOWS.

Great Glen Trails in Pinkham Notch has well-maintained trails, a complete rental center, lessons, and "baby carriage" sleds to pull along behind as you ski; 603-466-2333.

Appalachian Mountain Club, in Pinkham Notch, has 30 miles of ungroomed cross-country trails, available to use free of charge; 603-466-2721.

OUTDOOR ACTIVITIES

You may have the feeling you've been there before as you first approach the skating pond at **Nestlenook Farm** on Dinsmore Road in Jackson Village. This scene is right out of a Victorian Christmas card and is so appealing that it finds its way into a lot of promotional brochures. A bridge arches over the narrowest part of a frozen lake, and a sleigh is pulled over it by a team of horses decked out in jingling bells. On the lake's surface are skaters, many in Victorian costume, and others sit on the slatted wooden benches along the shore. The whole scene, under its backdrop of mountains is almost too perfect. The experience, which costs only $6 for a whole day of skating (plus $8 if you need to rent skates), is further enhanced by old-fashioned skating music, hot chocolate in front of an island, and lights around the lake at night. We can't think of another place that combines the fun of outdoor skating with such tastefully created Victorian-style elegance; 603-383-0845.

For parents who would prefer to sit inside comfortably

and watch their children pirouette on the ice, **Great Glen Trails** in Pinkham Notch has a new timber-frame base lodge with a restaurant, and full bar, in case a hot toddy sounds good. Skate rentals and floodlights at night add to its appeal; 603-466-2333.

Instead of skating, or as an interlude to rest your ankles, you can take a **sleigh ride** in an Austrian sleigh as it tours the trails of **Nestlenook's** 65-acre estate. The trails lead along the Ellis River and through the woods, past the Victorian inn, and includes a stop to visit reindeer. Percherons or English Shire horses pull the sleigh on its 30-minute rides. For a romantic ride for two or four, complete with champagne and fur blankets, choose the one-horse open sleigh, which costs about $100 for a couple or $120 for four. Sleigh rides are popular, so it's wise to reserve ahead; 603-383-0845.

Sleigh rides are also available at **Black Mountain Ski Area**, along with **dog sled rides** for children; 603-383-4490 or 800-475-4669.

Great Glen Trails is a new outdoor sports center near the base of the Mount Washington Auto Road in Pinkham Notch. Their trails are graded and maintained for both cross country skiers and those who prefer **snowshoeing.** A good selection of snowshoes is on hand for rental, and they offer inexpensive snowshoe clinics for those who feel more secure taking a lesson; 603-466-2333. **Nestlenook Farm** also has snowshoe trails and rents snowshoes; 603-383-0845.

The Appalachian Mountain Club, north of Jackson in Pinkham Notch, conducts frequent workshops to teach beginners the techniques of walking and climbing on **snowshoes.** They also offer programs on winter orienteering, so you won't get lost if you decide to explore off the established trails. These are two-day programs, and snowshoe rental is included in the fee. You'll trek to the Carter Notch hut, and the Club provides you with winter sleeping bags and backpacks, but it's up to you to carry in the food and bedding. Another program last five days: you'll spend the first two days on short trips, returning to the Crawford Hostel each night. The last two nights are spent at Zealand Falls Hut, after a day's hike along the frozen bed of the Zealand River. The fee (about $300) covers lodging, meals, instruction and use of equipment. The AMC also offers a series of weekend snowshoe adventures for families, a women's trek, and weekends for teens, as well as a weekend of wild animal tracking and observation on snowshoes. All programs require reservations; 603-466-2727.

Kick sledding is rarely seen here, but is a popular form of travel and recreation in Finland and other Arctic countries, where it's common to see housewives returning home with their groceries safely stowed on the back of a kick sled. They work much like a scooter, but with runners, not wheels. They are easy to operate, with one foot on the sled at all times and the other taking occasional long pushing steps to keep the sled moving. **Great Glen Trails** has both the sleds and the trails to ride them on, providing a unique opportunity to try these European favorites; 603-466-2333.

The Appalachian Mountain Club has three-day intensive courses in **ice climbing**, which include lodging and meals as well as use of all necessary equipment. A separate course is available for women, although women are also welcome in the general course. Men do not have a separate course of their own; 603-466-2727.

The Appalachian Mountain Club also offers courses and workshops on a variety of **winter skills**, such as **mountaineering**, recognizing and avoiding avalanches, **animal tracking, winter ecology, winter weather, photographing** the frozen landscape, and winter rescue and **survival** techniques. These are all held at the club's headquarters in Pinkham Notch or the Crawford Notch Hostel. They are graded for skill levels and vary in length from a weekend to a week, although most last one weekend. The cost for most weekend programs, without meals or lodging, is about $80. The club also offers shorter programs at a minimal fee, including shelter-building and animal tracking. A schedule is available; 603-466-2727.

A chance to learn the ancient craft of **igloo and snow shelter building** is rare enough, but to build one and actually camp overnight in it is even more unusual. The AMC offers this opportunity one weekend each winter, beginning with a classroom session on Friday evening. On Saturday, participants don snowshoes and put the theory into practice, building igloos, snow shelters or snow caves, as the weather conditions dictate. They cook supper at their winter campsite and sleep overnight in the shelters they've built. The whole experience, including meals, costs about $130; 603-466-2727.

Several **winter camping** workshops are held each winter, lasting from three to five days. You'll camp out and receive instruction in meal planning and cooking in cold weather, heat management and comfort, and using a tent in the snow. Other trips emphasize winter backpack travel and use the AMC huts for lodging; 603-466-2727.

Dog sledding trips with the AMC do require you to be a competent cross-country skier, but it is such a unique and exciting opportunity that we are including it for those who are comfortable on Nordic trails. You'll spend the weekend with a team of Alaska-trained dogs, learn dog-team handling and take turns mushing. Your gear travels on their sleds, so you can travel with a light daypack and enjoy the scenery. Lodging is in winter tents with portable woodstoves. Outdoor expedition clothing and snowshoes for use at the campsite are provided, but you must reserve them in advance; 603-466-2727.

If you want to ignore winter entirely and think ahead to spring and summer, you can learn the delicate craft of **tying fishing flies** in a weekend course given by the AMC. Along with gaining a familiarity with materials, you'll tie a variety of different flies. You can bring your own tools or buy a kit at the workshop; 603-466-2727.

EVENTS

December: **Traditionally Yours, Jackson** is held on the last weekend in November and the first two in December. The event begins with the arrival of Santa in a horse-drawn sleigh and an open house at a local restaurant. Admission is a modest donation to local charities. A **chocolate tour** via horse and wagon visits local inns, where you can sample their best chocolate creations. A **jazz breakfast, Christmas ornament workshops, cooking classes, a sing-along and hayride** for children, **hayrides** through the village, and **free ice skating** at Nestlenook Farm complete the weekend; 603-383-9356 or 800-866-3334.

Mid-January: **Jackson Winter Carnival** is an entire week filled with entertainment, **cooking workshops**, **ice carving** and **snow sculpture** contests, **parades, fireworks, music, snowshoe tours, a kids' pizza carnival, sleigh rides, ice skating** and **fondue parties**; 603-383-9356 or 800-866-3334.

Mid-January: The **Northern New Hampshire Winterfest Celebration** includes the three towns of Berlin, Gorham and Shelburne in a long weekend of winter activities. A **bonfire, sleigh rides, a snowshoe trek, a broomball tournament, maple sugar on snow, ice and snow sculptures** and more take place throughout this area just north of Pinkham Notch. Broomball, by the way, is like hockey with sneakers, brooms and balls instead of skates, sticks and hockey pucks; 603-752-6060.

WHERE TO CURL UP BY THE FIRE

The Inn at Thorn Hill, designed by Stanford White, is one of the loveliest properties in a town known for its many fine summer homes that have been converted into inns. Rooms have fireplaces, views are magnificent, and the dining room is one of the North Country's best. Relax in the outdoor hot tub, go for a sleigh ride, or just enjoy the antiques-filled atmosphere of the inn itself. The dining room is one of the best in the White Mountains. The inn is on Thorn Hill Road; 800-289-8990.

Wentworth Resort Hotel, in the center of Jackson Village, is a grand Victorian hotel with detached "cottages" built by wealthy city families who moved their households north for the summers. After a period of declining condition, the hotel and cottages were rescued just in time, completely restored, and greatly improved. The current owners have continued the process, adding whirlpool baths, custom-built furniture and numerous thoughtful details. Their love for the Wentworth really shows; the hallmarks of owner-management are evident throughout the property. The dining room is outstanding. For its level of luxury, its rates are surprisingly affordable; 603-383-9700 or 800-637-0013.

Whitney's Inn, at Black Mountain Ski Area (on Route 16-B 1-1/2 miles out of Jackson Village), is a relaxed family ski lodge, where everyone feels right at home. The property is well-maintained but not all dolled up. Some rooms have fireplaces. Recreation areas provide a good place for young people to congregate. Family-sized suites are a very attractive option, since children under 12 stay and eat free; 603-383-8916 or 800-677-5737.

Contemporary-styled condominiums at **Nordic Village** have fireplaces, double whirlpool baths, fully equipped kitchens and cable TV. Along with a swimming pool are a steam room and therapy spa. An outdoor skating rink has skating parties with bonfires. This is a luxury resort six miles north of North Conway, a mile north of Storyland; 603-383-9101 or 800-472-5207.

The Appalachian Mountain Club has private rooms and bunk space available in the Pinkham Notch facility. Linens are provided and hearty meals are served in a friendly, family-style setting. A common area with fireplace, a library and an information center provide a chance to learn about the trails and other outdoor activities available in the area; 603-466-2727.

Storybook Resort Inn, south of Jackson Village near the junction of Routes 16 and 302, is a family-run motel and inn with a restaurant. Its motel-style units have refrigerators and microwave ovens, while rooms in the inn are more old-fashioned, but equally comfortable. They are known for their breakfasts, with breads baked fresh daily; 603-383-6800 or 800-528-1234.

DINING

Highlights of the Jackson restaurant scene are the respective dining rooms at the **Wentworth Resort** and **The Inn at Thorn Hill**. Both are upscale and sophisticated, with menus that frequently border on inspired. Menus change seasonally, as the chefs take advantage of whatever is freshest. We group these two outstanding restaurants together because we can't imagine a visit to Jackson that doesn't allow an evening to dine in each. The Wentworth Resort phone is 603-383-9700; Thorn Hill is 603-383-4242.

Whitney's remembers its role as a family resort very well, with a child-friendly atmosphere and menu selections, while still offering a lively menu for adults. The dining room here is not the average family restaurant, and is well worth the mile-and-a-half trip from the village; 603-383-8916.

Thompson House Eatery, in the center of the village, is an Italian restaurant specializing in seafood. An old-fashioned soda fountain is a highlight of the decor; 603-383-9341.

Wildcat Inn and Tavern serves an eclectic menu in an old New England inn atmosphere. Specialties are Lobster Lorenzo and Long Island duck, and daily specials always include veal, beef and seafood; 603-383-4245.

NORTH OF THE NOTCHES: CANNON MOUNTAIN AND BRETTON WOODS

This area is roughly bounded by Routes 2 and 302, and extends from Bretton Woods to Cannon Mountain. The largest town is Littleton. Close by is Bethlehem, one of the earliest White Mountain resort towns, which once had dozens of grand summer hotels, including the Maplewood, whose huge stone casino you can't miss. Notice the variety in architectural styles along the main street; Bethlehem is thought to have more examples of different styles than any other town its size in New England.

Nearby, Sugar Hill stretches along a scenic maple-tree crowned hillside. During the Golden Age of the resort hotels, Sugar Hill was one of the most fashionable resort towns in New England. The drive along Route 117, especially heading east, offers some of the best mountain views.

Route 117 ends in Franconia, once the home of Robert Frost. You can see his farm on the Easton Road (Route 116); look on the right for a modest farmhouse and its mailbox, labeled *R. Frost*. Also in Franconia, and even easier to spot in the winter when it stands out in contrast to the white landscape, is the last remaining **iron furnace** in the state, one of the best preserved in New England. The giant stone tower stands across the river, where iron ore from Sugar Hill was smelted until 1850. Look for it across the river, near the Lafayette Regional School.

The Franconia/Sugar Hill area is a good base for lodgings, not only because of the wide choice available, but because of its central location to a number of attractions.

For further information on the area north of the notches, contact the Twin Mountain Chamber of Commerce, Twin Mountain, NH 03595; 603-846-5407 or

800-245-TWIN for lodging. Or contact The White Mountain Attractions Association at P.O. Box 10, North Woodstock, NH 03262; 603-745-8720 or 800-FIND-MTS.

FOR THOSE WHO SKI

Cannon Mountain in Franconia Notch is one of the earliest ski areas in the U.S. Like Cranmore's Skimobile, Cannon's tramway revolutionized the way skiers got to the top of the mountain. Unlike the skimobile, the tramway is still there, though its cars are bigger now. It's still one of the most enjoyable rides in the White Mountains. Its 2146-foot vertical drop is the steepest and most expert in the state; the view from any trail is spectacular. Cannon is a challenging area for serious skiers, 603-823-5563.

Bretton Woods is a family ski area with 32 trails, night skiing, and a cross-country center on the grounds of the famous Mount Washington Hotel. In fact, the impressive Victorian stables near the hotel become the cross-country center when snow flies. Ski school, nursery, pre-ski programs, and frequent kids' events make the area popular with parents of small children; 603-278-5000 or 800-232-2972.

Across the road, almost in the shadow of the grand Mount Washington Hotel, is the **Bretton Woods Cross Country Center**, with 50 miles of trails with mountain views all around; 603-278-5181. **Franconia Inn**, in the village of Franconia, has over 35 miles of cross-country trails on the valley floor; 603-823-5542. In nearby Sugar Hill, **Sunset Hill House** has about the same amount of trails on a high ridge. The views from the town of Sugar Hill are some of the best in the mountains; 603-823-5522.

OUTDOOR ACTIVITIES

The **Bretton Woods Cross Country Center** rents **snowshoes**, and the entire valley and the adjoining

National Forest are traversed by trails that beg to be explored; 603-278-5181.

At the northern end of **Franconia Notch** is the **Aerial Tramway**, which carries skiers to the top of Cannon Mountain, but you don't have to ski to ride up and see the views that reach all the way to Canada. The restaurant at the top of the tramway is crowded with skiers on weekends.

From the parking lot for the Aerial Tramway, you can take the short trail to Echo Lake for a good view of the state's symbol, the **Old Man of the Mountain**. This stone profile is made up of three separate ledges, which from below appear as one craggy face.

The Rocks, a nineteenth-century estate farm in Bethlehem, has marked trails through the farmland, woodlots and Christmas tree plantation. The barns and outbuildings were built from stone cleared from the rocky fields. Year-round activities here highlight the responsible uses of the land. Their Christmas tree plantation is open during December; 603-444-6228.

INDOOR ACTIVITIES

At the base of the Aerial Tramway is the **New England Ski Museum**, which you can easily spot by the car from the original tramway standing in front of it. The museum contains early equipment, Olympic memorabilia and other displays on every facet of skiing from The Mountain Division and Ski Troopers in the military to the history of skiwear. Vintage skiing films are shown continuously. It's open Thursday through Tuesday, and there is no admission charge; 603-823-7177.

Christie's Maple Farm on Route 2 in Lancaster is a working sugarhouse, which welcomes visitors and offers samples as they watch the sap boiling into syrup. Sugaring season begins in mid-March, but the sugarhouse is also open in December; 603-788-4118.

EVENTS

Late November: The Willing Workers **Christmas Sale** in Sugar Hill is not just another holiday bazaar. Like everything else that happens in this town, it is out of the ordinary. Look here for fine handiwork and unusual crafts, as well as one-of-a-kind foods; 603-823-9507.

Early December: **Christmas in Bethlehem** is a town-wide commemoration of its founding on Christmas Day. B&Bs open for tours and feature a different theme each year—one year it was gingerbread houses—with demonstrations. The Post Office issues a special cachet cover, and you can buy balsam wreaths and trees at the Rocks Estate. Bethlehem is on Route 302 east of Littleton. Hours are 1-4 p.m. on Saturday and Sunday and tickets are about $10; 603-869-3409.

Mid-February: School vacation week is celebrated in Franconia with the **Frostbite Follies**, with festivities ranging from dances and skating parties to a torchlight parade down the trails of Cannon Mountain; 603-823-5655.

Early March: Littleton is the scene of the Northern U.S. National **Sled Dog Races**; 603-444-6561.

Early April: Cannon Mountain's **April-Fest Celebration** is filled with silly snow activities and games. Things like this happen up here after a long winter; 603-823-5563.

SHOPPING AND CRAFTS

Harman's Cheese and Country Store in Sugar Hill sells fine aged cheddar cheese, which they ship to devotees the world over, as well as maple syrup, jams and jellies and other specialty foods. They are open Monday through Saturday; 603-823-8000.

While in Sugar Hill, stop at **P.C. Anderson Handmade Furniture** on Center District Road. Made of solid hardwood throughout, Peter's furniture is both beautiful and built to last. The studio is open 9-5 daily, but it's wise to call ahead before traveling any distance; 603-823-5209.

Antique shops are often closed in the winter, but **Potato Barn Antiques Center**, a large group shop in Lancaster, is open Friday-Sunday from January through March. In November and December it is open daily. Look here for items relating to the White Mountains, including souvenirs of the long-gone grand hotels that once filled the area. There is quite a variety here, with larger items downstairs; prices are moderate, with some real bargains hiding in the corners, especially if you are used to city prices; 603-636-2611.

A handful of the antique shops in Bethlehem remain open through the winter as well. Some are open only weekends, a couple on selected weekdays.

Where To Curl Up By The Fire

The Mount Washington Hotel, at Bretton Woods, celebrates the completion of its first century of operation by extending its season to twelve months. Now open all year, the hotel is newly insulated, with heating installed, to offer a warm welcome to skiers and those who want to pretend it's still summer and never set foot outdoors. Guests have included presidents, prime ministers and crowned heads of state; in fact, the hotel's most flamboyant owner was a princess. Free public tours go behind the scenes and show why this landmark has endured as the others have disappeared one by one. Winter weekend activities include Mardi Gras, a winter carnival, St. Patrick's Day, food expositions, and music festivals; 603-278-1000 or 800-258-0330.

The Bretton Arms is part of the Mount Washington Hotel property, and a historic landmark in its own right. It is a country inn with large, bright, well-decorated rooms and an outstanding dining room, located only a few yards from the cross-country skiing center. Entertainment on weekends may be a Celtic balladeer; don't miss the chance to take a **sleigh ride** around the Mount Washington Hotel for superb views of the Presidential Range and the grand hotel itself; 603-278-1000 or 800-258-0330.

Perched on the top of what we think is the most scenic ridge in the White Mountains, **Sunset Hill House** is in the town of Sugar Hill, almost straight up from the town of Franconia. The last remaining building of what was once a grand summer hotel, the inn has been completely restored with all the modern comforts added. Nearly 20 miles of cross-country trails run through light woods and along the ridge, beginning at the door, which are freshly groomed each morning while you're eating breakfast. The inn also offers horse-drawn sleigh rides, snowshoeing, tobogganing, and plenty of places to settle in with a good book. Plan to be at an east-facing window just after sunset, when the sky reflects onto the snow-covered mountains in the rosiest alpenglow we've seen this side of Austria. A long-standing tradition here is their **Thanksgiving weekend work bee**, when inn guests pitch in with the innkeepers (a good-humored and energetic family team) to decorate the inn for the holidays, bring in the winter wood, and tend to other seasonal chores. It is so much fun that many of the guests have been coming for years; 603-823-5522 or 800-SUN-HILL.

We've recommended the **Hilltop Inn**, on Route 117 in the center of Sugar Hill, to so many friends that we're afraid they won't have room for us next time we call. Antique and custom-crafted furnishings blend in a decor with a sense of humor and a keen eye to the details that make a room comfortable: big pillows, good lights for bedtime reading, and warm quilts. Merri, one of the pair of innkeepers who gives Hilltop Inn its air of easy grace, is a talented chef, so breakfasts are memorable. So is the lively atmosphere and conversation. Children are welcome here, as are pets; 603-823-5695 or 800-770-5695.

Sugar Hill Inn, on Route 117 in Sugar Hill, overlooks the mountains with warm, inviting rooms. Victorian bathtubs, well-chosen art, and friendly hosts set this inn apart. So does the dining room, for guests only, and only on weekends; 603-823-5621.

The most avid skier will have trouble leaving the luxuries of **Adair** for a day on the slopes. It makes no pretense of being anything but a classy place to be pampered. The house is just right for it, a mansion built by an eminent trial lawyer as a wedding gift for his daughter in 1927. Frederick Law Olmstead designed the gardens (you'll have to return in the summer to see these) and the estate's grounds total over 200 acres. Guest rooms are furnished in antiques and fine reproductions and decorated with original art. Most have mountain views. Pool enthusiasts will enjoy using the fine old Oliver Briggs Boston table in the Tap Room downstairs. Afternoon tea is served daily at 4. Fireplaces give a cozy feeling, while large windows seem to bring the white outdoor landscapes inside. Adair is not the Real World, and it doesn't want to be; 603-444-2600 or 888-444-2600.

DINING

For dinner with a view, plus a free ride on the chairlift, reserve a table at **Top o' the Quad**, the casual restaurant on the mountainside of Bretton Woods Ski Area. They even supply blankets for the chilly ride up. Or you can take the free van. During the day this is the summit lodge and lunchroom for skiers; 603-278-5000.

Italian Oasis, in downtown Littleton, leads a Jekyll and Hyde existence as a brew pub/Italian restaurant. The two blend well, with the restaurant's lunch menu doubling as a tavern menu. All the red-sauce favorites—manicotti, ravioli, veal parmesan, chicken cacciatore—are served in a bright glass-enclosed room. The tiny brewery's ale—they brew only 62 gallons at a time—are served in the pub with 14 others; 603-444-6995.

Dinner at **The Bretton Arms**, on the property of the Mount Washington Hotel, is a first-rate dining experience. Begin with Vermont cheddar and walnut ravioli or hickory smoked duck, tender and delicately flavored, or a wild mushroom and dried tomato soup. From there it's a close choice between the salmon and the lamb, each of which is unfailingly cooked to exactly the right second; 603-278-1000.

   Tim-Bir Alley, at **Adair** in Bethlehem, serves some of the finest dinners in the western White Mountains. Delightful flavor combinations of quality ingredients may pair old favorites or introduce two total culinary strangers, such as duck and figs. Dinners are by reservations only; 603-444-4823.

THE BALSAMS WILDERNESS

Perhaps we should begin by saying that really serious skiers—the kind who look at the vertical drop when choosing a mountain—don't go to **The Balsams Wilderness**. But a lot of others do, if not for the challenge of its slopes, then for the whole outdoors and indoors experience it offers. The Balsams is, to us, the epitome of what winter in New England is all about.

It is a first-class resort hotel of the old school on the American plan, with no extra charges for activities—even skiing—and a self-contained place to spend a winter vacation. It doesn't just *have* all the activities that make the outdoors appealing in winter, it *lives* them. Set deep in the woods in a wonderland setting midway up New Hampshire's narrowest and northernmost notch, it has to be self-contained because it's a long way to the nearest anything else.

But it is also self-sufficient, producing its own heat, its own maple syrup, its own crystal-clear spring water, and its own entertainment. Snowshoeing, ice skating, winter nature hikes, stargazing, and wildlife watching are all part of the north country way of life, and you can easily become part of it. The concierge is an expert woodsman, the bellman can suggest a good snowshoe trail, and your waiter is likely to know when the meteor showers are.

The service is professional, but interested; nearly everyone has worked there for years and feels a proprietary sense about the hotel. The executive chef is among New England's finest and his staff is given every encouragement to create original dishes. It's not by chance that students who have trained at the Balsams are now chefs at some of New England's finest restaurants. In the winter the rate includes their enormous buffet breakfast and a multi-course dinner. While it isn't cheap, as a vacation package with all activities included, it's hard to beat.

This is no rustic lodge, despite its general air of outdoorsiness. It is a grand hotel, and its food, service and facilities are a match for any resort anywhere; along with the cross-country and snowshoe trails, they include the indoor pleasures of a movie theater, ping-pong, billiards, board games, live entertainment, musical performances, lectures, and nature programs. But the most memorable thing about The Balsams is that the people there are real, not a bunch of Stepford wives with painted-on smiles and memorized welcome spiels.

The Balsams Wilderness also has about 45 miles of groomed cross-country trails through scenic woods and fields, much of which is lighted for night skiing. The ski area is ideal for families, with a good ski school and an easy-going air of people enjoying themselves; 800-255-0800 in New Hampshire, 800-255-0600 elsewhere.

For information on other events and activities in the far north, contact the Connecticut Lakes Tourist Association, P.O. Box 38, Pittsburg, NH 03592.

OUTDOOR ACTIVITIES

Snowmobiles are more than a sport here, they are the only way to get to certain places in the wintertime. **Pathfinder Sno-Tours and Rentals** is located at Timberland Lodge on the First Connecticut Lake in Pittsburg, and they offer guided tours of the vast coniferous forests and lakes that stretch to the Canadian border; 603-538-6613 for Timberland Lodge, 603-538-7001 for tours..

Snowmobile repair and service is offered by Granite State Power Equipment on Route 3 in Pittsburg; 603-538-6349.

WHERE TO CURL UP BY THE FIRE

Although The Balsams is the focal point of the Dixville Notch area and has the great majority of available lodging, a few other options are open in the winter.

Timberland Lodge and Cabins, on the First Connecticut Lake in Pittsburg, has 21 cabins on the lake, each with woodstove and automatic heat. They provide the wood. **Snowmobile** trails leave from the door and **ice fishing** is a few steps away; 603-538-6613 or 800-545-6613.

Rooms With a View has just what it claims, mountains from every window. Rooms are cozy, with hand-pieced quilts, sheepskin bathmats and other warming touches. Breakfast bread is baked in the huge ceramic stove in the kitchen; 603-237-5106 or 800-499-5106.

MAINE

It's only fair. Maine shares a bit of its abundant seacoast with New Hampshire while New Hampshire allows some of its White Mountains to run over the border into Maine. Good neighbors share things like that. Maine's prime ski country isn't very broad, and the distance from major urban populations has kept the area from being overcrowded with ski resorts. But quality makes up for quantity, and four mountains literally stand out above the rest. They are all in the region Maine calls The Western Lakes and Mountains.

Skiing is still a fairly new industry in Maine, despite the state-of-the-art facilities at Sugarloaf, which was popular with serious skiers back as far as the sixties. Winter sports, primarily snowmobiling and ice fishing, still reign supreme. Winter visitors will find a total of 10,500 miles of maintained snowmobile trails in the state. A non-resident fee of $35-60 is required to use these, a real bargain when you consider the quantity and variety of trails that are available to you. For more information on snowmobiling, call the Maine Snowmobile Association at 207-622-6983.

Maine's White Mountains begin at the New Hampshire border with Bethel. Almost directly north is Rangeley, better known for its lakes than its mountains. To the east is Kingfield and Carrabassett Valley, a new and thriving town that has been created close to Sugarloaf. Between Bethel and Kingfield, on Route 2, is Farmington, which gave the earmuff to the world. They celebrate this invention each December on Chester Greenwood Day.

For a free guide to winter activities throughout the state, call 800-440-2248 weekdays. For up-to-date reports on snowmobiling conditions in each area, call 800-880-SNOW.

SUNDAY RIVER AND BETHEL

Bethel looks like the prototype of a classic small New England town, with fine clapboard homes and a white-spired church set around a green at the top of a hill. It is home to Gould Academy, a private boarding school which adds more cultural events than a town this size would be able to support otherwise. That, in turn, attracts people who support the arts, the local historical society, and other community affairs. It's every bit nice a town as it appears to be, and travelers will find gracious lodging and good dining here.

Most of the development is confined to the surrounding mountains, convenient for skiers and sports enthusiasts, but near enough to town so that visitors have the option of a village instead of slopeside base.

For information on Maine's Western Mountains, contact the Bethel Area Chamber of Commerce, P.O. Box 439, Bethel, ME 04217.

FOR THOSE WHO SKI

Sunday River has Maine's second greatest vertical drop, at 2340 feet, and is covered with more than 126 trails evenly divided among skill levels. With more than 30 expert trails, it is a favorite with serious skiers. Eighteen chairlifts on eight mountains keep lines at a minimum; 207-824-3000.

Sunday River Cross Country Ski Center has nearly 20 miles of groomed trails plus backcountry skiing; 207-824-2410. **Bethel Inn Ski Touring Center** has 20 miles of groomed trails, and unlimited skiing on their 200-acre golf course; 207-824-6276.

Telemark Inn, in West Bethel, puts a new spin on cross-country skiing by crossing it with dog sledding. You are the sled, with your skis as the runners, pulled through the woods and over the fields by a couple of excited huskies. It's called **ski joring**, and you can try it or **cross-country skiing** at the inn's ski center. Begin with a two-hour private lesson; 207-836-2703.

OUTDOOR ACTIVITIES

Hurricane Island Outward Bound is located on the road paralleling Route 27 north of the Sunday River access road, and offers an enticing choice of winter programs. These are designed for enjoyment, not just survival training, and for all ages and experience levels. The center provides packs, parkas, sleeping bags, and other winter equipment the average person might not have on hand, all geared towards showing you how comfortable you can be outdoors, even in a severe climate like northern Maine's. Although they will conduct events for groups, most of their programs are made up of people who have signed up individually.

Snowshoeing instruction and guided hikes are a popular feature of Outward Bound's winter calendar. Some of these trips include **winter camping**, where participants set up a campsite and cook meals in the woods after hiking in on snowshoes; 800-341-1744.

Those who prefer to be accompanied into the backwoods by the howl and yip of dogs instead of the hum of a motor, can learn the art of mushing on a **dogsled safari**. Fully outfitted day or longer trips allow you to handle your own team or just enjoy the ride. Meals and all gear are provided by **Mahoosuc Guide Service** in Newry, just north of Bethel; 207-824-2073. Outward Bound offers eight-day dogsled adventures; 800-341-1744.

Ice climbing lessons include classroom sessions at the **Outward Bound Center**, where you can learn the ropes, literally, before coming to grips with an icy mountain face. This program is open only to those who are 18 or older, and a medical form is required; 800-341-1744.

Snowmobiles are a common sight around Bethel, with trails leading into the White Mountain National

Forest. Sun Valley Sports on the Sunday River Road rents snowmobiles; 207-824-7553.

The town of Bethel maintains a **skating rink** on the Common which visitors are welcome to use.

INDOOR ACTIVITIES

We have avoided suggesting places that are open only by appointment in the winter, but the people at Bethel Historical Society are so accommodating and happy to show their **Moses Mason House** that we know they'd be disappointed if we didn't mention it. Nine period rooms are furnished to reflect the lives and times of Dr. and Mrs. Mason, both prominent figures in Maine history. The house, which was built in 1813, is decorated with murals thought to be by Rufus Porter. To arrange a time for a tour of the house, call 207-824-2908.

EVENTS

December: Christmas in the Valley fills the towns of Rumford, Mexico and Dixfield with fairs, sleigh rides and other seasonal festivities; 207-364-3241.

Late December: Mount Abrams Ski Area in Locke Mills has a torchlight parade of skiers and a party; 207-875-5003.

Mid-February: Mushers Bowl, on Moose Pond in West Bridgeton, south of Bethel, with more than 50 dogsled teams; 207-539-4324.

February: Sunday River Ski Area Mardi Gras, featuring costume ball, torchlight parade, fireworks and Cajun foods; 207-824-3000.

First Saturday in April: Sunday River Cross Country Center hosts **Pole, Paddle and Paw**, a combination ski, snowshoe and canoe event for teams or individuals; 207-824-2410.

Shopping and Crafts

Western Maine has an abundance of gems and semiprecious stones hiding in its rocks; it is a prime hunting ground for rock hounds. **Mount Mann Jewelers** in Main Street Place, mines, cuts and sets these Maine stones into fine jewelry. You'll find tastefully set amethyst, aquamarine and watermelon tourmaline, along with beryl and other high quality gems; 207-824-3030.

For books on Maine, especially its history, browse in **Books 'n Things** on Main Street in Bethel. It is a general-interest bookstore as well, with best sellers, whodunits for fireside reading on a stormy night and stories to read to the kids; 207-824-0275.

Where To Curl Up By The Fire

Bethel Inn and Country Club, in a classic New England village setting overlooking the green (or in winter, the *white*), has a full health club with a heated outdoor pool, saunas, and traditional inn rooms or condo-style suites. Rooms in the inn are furnished with quality antique reproductions. It looks like the quintessential New England Inn, and it is, but with resort facilities; 207-824-2175 or 800-654-0125.

Slopeside condos at Sunday River are convenient to the ski area and its facilities, including restaurants. Units are small, but equipped with full kitchens. Expect a friendly staff and a large swimming pool; 800-543-SKI.

Abbott House has finally done what we've wished for in a lot of B&Bs after a day on snowshoes: they have a resident massage therapist. With this and a hot tub, you don't even need their extra-comfortable beds for a good night's sleep. This 18th-century cape, one-half mile from the edge of the village, is beautifully kept; 207-824-7600 or 800-240-2377.

L'Auberge Country Inn, just off the Bethel common, has guest rooms and serves dinners of fresh seafood, game and choice cuts in a refined casual atmosphere, but to overnight guests only; 207-824-2774 or 800-760-2774.

DINING

The Bethel Inn and Country Club, right in the center of town, sets the stage with glowing fireplaces and music on the Steinway. Children under 11 eat free at 5:30, then are treated to a movie while parents relax over a leisurely dinner of prime rib, duckling or swordfish; 207-824-2175.

Sunday River Brewing Company, at the corner of the Sunday River access road, serves lunch and dinner to go with its fresh ales. They also give tours of their microbrewery. It's open every day, with live music three nights a week; 207-824-4ALE.

Pizzas baked in a wood-fired oven are the specialty of **The Matterhorn** on Lower Main Street in Bethel; 207-824-OVEN.

SADDLEBACK AND RANGELEY

We've always been fond of the Rangeley area; we've been lost looking for more waterfalls here than in any other part of New England. Not that local people don't give good directions—they are so friendly that they may offer to take you there themselves—it's just that it's easy to miss the fifth woods road on the left, or mistake it for a driveway. Some of these waterfalls are spectacular and approachable in the winter, albeit carefully, so do ask your innkeeper.

Rangeley Lake dominates the town. Its frozen expanse simply expands the town in winter, when it becomes a busy highway for snowmobiles and a miniature village of bobhouses. Along with rustic cabins and camps you'll find fine inn accommodations and at least one very good dining room in town. Contact Rangeley Lakes Chamber of Commerce, P.O. Box 317, Rangeley, ME 04970; 207-864-5571. For lodging reservations call 800-MT-LAKES.

FOR THOSE WHO SKI

Saddleback Mountain has 1800 feet of vertical drop, with trails in all skill levels served by two double chair lifts and three T-bars; 207-864-5671.

Saddleback's **Ski Nordic** center has an elevation of over 2,000 feet, so good snow conditions last well into spring. Fifty miles of trails are adjacent to the downhill area; 207-864-5671. Rangeley's municipal trails include 12 miles of groomed trails, and over 150 of backcountry and snowmobile trails; 207-864-3326.

OUTDOOR ACTIVITIES

Snowmobiling is the national sport here, with more than 150 miles of well-maintained trails, complete with trailside services. Trails connect to the 260-mile international circuit into Quebec. Trails are so well-marked that you don't have to be familiar with them in order to ride safely, and detailed maps are available at many local shops. Lodging, food and service stations are located right on the trails. An active Snowmobile Club hosts public suppers the second Saturday of each month; 207-864-3326. Dockside Sports Center rents and services machines; 207-864-2424. Rivers Edge in Oquossoc rents snowmobiles and leads guided snowmobile tours; 207-864-5582.

EVENTS

Early December: **Walk to Bethlehem** is an evening of pageantry, community spirit and caroling in Rangeley. It's the kind of heartwarming (although nose-chilling, since much of it is out of doors) tradition that only a town the size and location of Rangeley could maintain; 207-864-4356.

January/February: A **torchlight parade** skis down Saddleback Mountain, beginning at the summit and ending at the base lodge; 207-864-5671.

Late January: Rangeley hosts a major **snowmobile race**, the Budweiser Snowmobile Snodeo, a festival complete with a parade, displays, games, and fireworks; 207-864-3368.

Early March: New England **Sled Dog Races** at Rangeley, with teams of all ages, including junior. Several teams race each day at the Rangeley Inn; 207-864-5364.

WHERE TO CURL UP BY THE FIRE

At **The Rangeley Inn**, don't worry if they don't have rooms in the main inn: those in the motel annex are not at all motel-like, and have picture windows overlooking the lake. Both hotel and motel rooms have whirlpool baths in modern bathrooms with large vanities and light bars, and fluffy thick towels. Victorian details like crystal doorknobs set on sculptured metal plates and brass corner pieces in stairways, characterize the main inn building. A feel for architecture has softened the visual impact of required emergency stairs at the back of the building by creating porches on each level overlooking the lake. Some units have refrigerators while others have fireplaces and king- or queen-sized beds. Energetic young innkeepers have breathed new life into this venerable classic overlooking the main street of town; 207-864-3341 or 800-MOMENTS.

Built as a private residence in 1912, **Northwoods** was always known as "the big house" in Rangeley. Now it is a B&B, and although a bit pricier than some other local options, it's in a class of its own with fine antiques and collections. Although it closes in November and December, the B&B is open from January through March; 207-864-2440 or 800-295-4968.

The soaring ceilings and great stone fireplaces of **Country Club Inn**'s lobby give a preview of its warm, pine-paneled rooms. Decor is simple and comfortable, with big windows to let the scenery in. The Country Club Inn is on Route 4, 1-1/2 miles from town; 207-864-3831.

Hunter Cove is a group of eight cabins on the shores of Rangeley Lake. Fully-equipped kitchens, lofts for extra people, hot tubs in a few, and ceiling fans in all make the cabins a cozy, private and practical alternative to a hotel. Each cabin has either a working fireplace or woodstove. Knotty pine walls and sturdy pine furniture give them a rustic alpine look; 207-864-3383.

The Horsefeather Inn sits right on a snowmobile trail, in the lakeside village of Oquossoc and prepares guests for the day ahead with a hearty sportsman's breakfast; 207-864-5465.

DINING

The Dining Room at The Rangeley Inn has meticulously restored wainscotting and high tin ceilings;

we don't know of another place that's taken so much care in restoring the wood finishes, which are so often painted. Large windows overlook Rangeley's main street. But for all the classic elegance, it's the food that brings us back: chicken Madeira, crabcakes with horseradish cream, shrimp with cherry tomatoes and black olives. All entrees, even lobster, are under $20; 207-864-3341.

Possibly the best value in town is at **The Red Onion**, where you will find a menu filled with home-style favorites such as liver and onions, baked manicotti, meatloaf, fried chicken and spaghetti; it's refreshing to see spaghetti on a menu in these days of fettuccine, penne and farfalle. The most expensive of these is $6.95. Pizzas are hand-built on their own fresh pizza dough: you buy the base and choose from 20 toppings; 207-864-5022.

SUGARLOAF AND CARRABASSETT VALLEY

Kingfield has been blessed in many ways throughout its history. First, it has benefited as the birthplace of the remarkable Stanley twins, whose family shared their success with their hometown, which accounts for some of its comely public buildings. More recently, the development of the Sugarloaf ski area has brought the prosperity of tourist money to the area, but without affecting the looks of the area's only town of any size. Most of the new construction is situated farther up Routes 16/27 nearer to the base of the mountain, in the newly-formed town of Carrabassett Valley. And because this town is very new, it, too, is attractive and well-kept, many of its buildings are designed in the stylish ski-modern architecture common to winter resorts all over New England. Farther north are Stratton and Eustis, both comfortably established villages.

Route 27 continues all the way to the Canadian border, through the towns of Eustis and Stratton. It's a scenic route to drive, especially when you get to Flagstaff Lake and the tall stand of Cathedral Pines, planted in the 1930s by the Civilian Conservation Corps.

For information on the area, contact Sugarloaf Area Chamber of Commerce, RR 1, Box 2151, Carrabassett Valley, ME 04947; 207-235-2100.

FOR THOSE WHO SKI

Sugarloaf's vertical rise of 2,820 feet make it the highest ski mountain in Maine, and its combination of summit snowfields, expert terrain, a three-mile run for intermediate skiers, and the gentle beginners area served by two chairlifts, make Sugarloaf a favorite for families. There really is plenty to do for everyone and the entire area is child-friendly with special deals and packages that add up to free skiing for kids. The entire resort is managed on a serious environmentally-conscious plan which affects everything from erosion control to snowmaking equipment; 800-THE-LOAF.

The **Sugarloaf Ski Touring Center** has more than 80 cross-country trails plus a solar-heated lodge that overlooks a moose bog and the alpine skiing slopes; 207-237-6830.

OUTDOOR ACTIVITIES

Sledding—the old-fashioned kind where you walk to the top of a neighbor's hill and slide down in whatever irregular path its bumps and gullies take you—is alive and well in Maine. If you want to share this impromptu pleasure with your children, or send them off by themselves (you won't find a much safer town), Gilmore's Hill is the place. On a sunny winter Saturday you'll find the hill peppered with bright roly-poly snowsuits in constant motion and alive with squeals and giggles. Ask anybody in town for directions. If you don't have a sled, you'll find them—and about anything else—at Anni's Market.

For those who like their sleds with motors, **snowmobiling** is a major sport in the valley, and it's not unusual to pull your car into Dick's Exxon and have to wait while three or four snowmobiles ahead of you fill up. The more than 300 miles of local trails are excellent and the local club, the Snow Wanderers, keeps them that way. The club welcomes new members to their monthly meetings and group rides; 207-265-4523. North of Carrabassett Valley, near Route 27, is a string of lakes and wild, open country with beautiful trails—and views—all the way into Canada. It's reminiscent of the Finnish Fells, but without the reindeer. You can rent snowmobiles for half or full days at Flagstaff Rentals in Stratton; 207-246-4276.

The Samoyeds at **T.A.D. Dog Sled Services** are the friendliest balls of white fur we've ever met, and they can't wait to get in front of a sled. Their obvious enjoyment of the whole process makes the dogsled rides even more fun. The trip is about two miles long and runs through the frozen woods, along the banks of the river and across open fields with fine mountain views. It lasts at least half an hour, maybe longer, and costs $35 for an adult and $25 for a child. Get a friend to go with you, since a single person in a sled must pay the $60 minimum for a ride. Lap robes keep you warm, but goggles or glasses are a good idea, since the dogs kick up a bit of snow as they run. A note to those who are allergic to dogs: Samoyeds do not carry the dander that causes allergic reaction. This is a popular activity, so it's best to call Tim Diehl for a reservation; 207-246-4461.

To learn the art of mushing, and drive your own sled into Maine's real backcountry, you can sign up for a fully outfitted trip at **The White Howling Express** in Stratton, north of Carrabassett Valley. Their trips are well-designed for families, providing the option to either drive a sled or ride along in the gear sleds. They bring snowshoes to use at the campsites and also provide all the necessary gear, as well as hearty meals; 207-246-4461.

Ice skating is available at Sugarloaf at the Ski Touring Center on a lighted Olympic-sized rink, where you can rent both hockey and figure skates; 207-237-6830.

Snowshoers use the trails at the Sugarloaf Ski Touring Center, which will rent snowshoes to visitors; access to the trails is free to people who rent snowshoes there; 207-237-6830.

INDOOR ACTIVITIES

Sugarloaf Sports and Fitness Club offers an indoor heated pool, indoor and outdoor hot tubs, a 25-station fitness center, sauna, steam room, ball courts, and indoor rock-climbing with professional instruction; 207-237-6946.

The Stanley twins enriched the world with a number of inventions, and the Stanley Steamer carried their name into history. They also pioneered early photographic techniques, and these two subjects make up much of the collections and exhibits at the **Stanley Museum** in Kingfield. Two Stanley Steamers are always on display at the museum, as are early cameras and an excellent exhibit explaining the various early photographic processes. Collectors of early games will enjoy the selection of games invented by the versatile Stanley family. It's open Tuesday through Sunday afternoons from 1-4, except in April and November, when it is closed, and a modest admission is charged; 207-265-2729.

There are few creatures more endearing than baby lambs, and **Sugarloaf Dorsets,** in Kingfield, has a barn full of them. Lambing takes place between January and March, so you are likely to be able to help bottle-feed one of these newborns, as well as watch those only a few weeks old gambol about in the hay. The barn is 150 feet long, and as you enter you will see the ribbons and awards—many of them quite prestigious—that the farm has earned with its Dorset herd. They've garnered four out of five best-in-breed awards in national competition, and you can even meet Sugarloaf, the 1994 National Sire of the Year. He's just a bit arthritic and moves a little slower now, which should be a lesson to all you young bucks out there. 150 years ago this was a working **sheep farm**, and thanks to a lot of hard work, it is again, with the pastures cleared to show sweeping mountain views. But in the winter, all the sheep are snug in their barn and you're welcome to see them any day from 9 to 5. To get to the farm, take Freeman Ridge Road off Route 27, opposite Kingfield Flooring, a tenth of a mile north of the county line marker; from there, it's one mile to the farm; 207-265-4549.

Nowetah's American Indian Museum on Route 27 in New Portland is the personal collection of an Abenaki woman who is dedicated to preserving the arts and ways of her ancestors through the museum and the programs she takes into local classrooms. Behind the small shop is a collection of historic and modern Indian-made baskets that any museum would kill for. Each is labeled with the artist's name and the year it was made, in addition to the materials and its intended use. Most are from the Abenaki, Micmac, Passamaquoddy or Penobscot groups. Both woven and birchbark baskets are included, the latter laced together with spruce root and decorated with carved and scraped designs. Look especially for the unusual woven birchbark apple-drying basket and the ear-of-corn basket carried in the Micmac corn planting dance. An equally impressive assortment of handwork and implements from tribes throughout the continent and some South American pieces make up the rest of the museum. The museum doesn't have an endowment and receives no public money. It was created and is kept open solely from the sales of the crafts they sell, which is also the family's sole source of income. Please remember this and be generous when you pass the very low-key container for contributions. Some of their work is museum-quality, and sold at amazing prices. A handwoven rug which takes eight months to make, for example, is only $260. Open 10-5, every day, all year, and admission is free; 207-628-4981.

Kids will enjoy the friendly **Western Maine Children's Museum** in the center of Carrabassett Valley, especially the Native American exhibit with a full-sized tepee. They can also see a beaver pond and climb aboard a real gondola from the ski area. The museum is open during the school year on Saturday, Sunday, and Monday year-round, 1-5. In an interesting twist, admission is $2.50 per child, but adults are free; 207-235-2211. The town's **public library** is located in the same building, and you're welcome to take out books while you're in the area. They will ask for a $5 deposit, which they return to you when you bring back the last book.

On The Way Between Bethel and Kingfield

Mainely Critters is a small private museum built by a husband-and-wife team of skilled taxidermists. As they are quick to point out, all the animals here were brought to them from highway accidents, and they have mounted them in natural attitudes, that are characteristic to the species as it goes about the everyday business of its life. A fawn nurses, otters cavort in a pond, and a young moose has pond weeds hanging like spaghetti from his mouth. It is an excellent opportunity for children—and adults—to see real animals close up in their natural settings. The museum is open all winter, wheelchair accessible and free. It is on Route 2, between Dixfield and Wilton; 207-562-8231.

EVENTS

December: **Chester Greenwood Day** celebrates his winter-changing invention of this Farmington native: the earmuff.

Late December: Sugarloaf's **Christmas Celebration** usually falls on the weekend before Christmas, with a torchlight parade of skiers, fireworks and the lighting of their big Christmas Tree; 207-237-2000.

January: **White World Week** is filled with parades, fireworks, concerts and a chili cook-off; 207-237-2000.

Mid-February: Sugarloaf Area Chamber of Commerce **Auction** features restaurant and lodging certificates and outdoor equipment; 207-235-2100.

Late February: **Farmington Winter Games**, with indoor and outdoor events from art shows and dances to snowsculpting contests, skating parties, snowmobile events, and an ice-fishing derby; 207-778-4215.

SHOPPING AND CRAFTS

Ritzo & Royall Studio Gallery shows the paintings and prints of artist Patty Ritzo, the stained glass of Jan Royall, and works of other artists in a variety of media. It's on Route 27 just north of the village in Kingfield and is open afternoons, Thursday through Sunday; 207-265-5626.

You can find **Kingfield Wood Products** by their tall

smokestacks. They make use of the product this part of the world has in ample supply: wood. (Sugarloaf Ski Area makes use of the other plentiful commodity around here: the snow.) The factory makes everything from clothespins to rolling pins, and their factory store always has an assortment of products at bargain prices. They are open Saturday and Sunday from 9-4; 207-265-2151.

Scent-Sations, at the Herbert Hotel in Kingfield, is filled with fragrant, healthy skin care products and perfume oils. Their unique perfume bar allows you to create your own personal blend from the dozens of oils they stock. Look for fine soaps, shampoos and bath luxuries as well; 207-265-4560.

A DAY EXCURSION

Although it's not right in the Valley, one of the most enjoyable ways to spend a day in the late winter is to travel into Canada to a sugar cabin, the maple farms that serve three meals a day for less than $10 a person, Canadian (currently about $7.50). Some are large and commercial, while others are small family-run sugarhouses, but the menu is nearly always the same: baked ham, boiled potatoes, chunky pommes frittes, baked beans, a tossed salad, coleslaw, platters of fried eggs or omelets, oeufs au neige (eggs poached in maple sap), fried pork rinds, homemade pickles and preserves, coffee, tea, and milk. Then comes dessert, individual crepes with maple syrup, sugar pie, and *Grandpere*, a yeast bread twist in maple syrup. And, of course, traditional sugar on snow. You eat a little of everything or pick what you like, and eat as much as you like. Plan at least an hour and a half for this congenial, family-style meal, and brush up on your *s'il vous plais*, since most of your fellow diners will be Quebecoise, not surprisingly, since you're in Quebec. You can choose from a number of sugar cabins—the activities office at the base of Sugarloaf can give you directions to them—but our favorite is a family-run place on a dirt road, called Cabine

Bellavance. Sugaring lasts late up there, as does ski season at Sugarloaf, so you can enjoy this trip throughout April and sometimes into May.

WHERE TO CURL UP BY THE FIRE

In most towns, **The Herbert** would seem like an anachronism, its big square freshly-painted frame sitting flush with Main Street, but in Kingfield this classic looks right at home. No run-down relic of the last century, this is a well-maintained hotel, its interior gleaming with fine wood paneling, its fireplace radiating warmth to the comfortable plush sofas that wait in front of it. Even the big moose head over the mantel—usually wearing a seasonally appropriate hat—looks friendly and good humored. There are no televisions or in-room phones to disturb the peace of this Beaux Arts hotel, but it's far from boring when the lively guests gather in the evening. It's not wholly without modern amenities, however: The Herbert does have Jacuzzis; 800-THE-HERB.

Winter's Hill Inn is located in a National Register mansion that overlooks the town's rooftops on one side and the mountains on the other. Antiques fill its rooms, but they don't interfere with guests' comfort; big, soft sofas and easy chairs mix easily with the historic pieces. Four guest rooms are in the original mansion, the rest in a barn. Cross-country ski trails leave from the backyard, and **Julia's** serves high-class meals in a lovely setting, a pleasure reserved for winter visitors to the valley, since Julia's is closed in the summer; 207-265-5421 or 800-233-9687.

The slopeside **condo units** at Sugarloaf are convenient and nicely appointed, with solid cherry paneling on the cabinets, working fireplaces, and Murphy beds to allow more living space in the already large rooms. Furniture is made from solid wood and is comfortable, with two couches and a dining table, as well as two bunks for extra people. The slope-facing end of each unit is solid glass with sliding doors that open onto a terrace or balcony. Kitchens include microwave ovens and coffee makers as well as roomy refrigerators. A pool and fitness center is located in the same building. These condos are among the nicest slopeside accommodations we've stayed in, and **The Sugarloaf Inn**, with restaurant, lounge, and common areas is just as pleasant.

All together, these slopeside accommodations can sleep more than 7,000 guests, but this part of the world is roomy enough so that it never feels crowded; 207-237-2000 or 800-THE-LOAF.

The Widow's Walk is a B&B in a Victorian home, fifteen minutes from the ski area. Rooms share baths, but the price is unbelievably low for such an elegant home. The owners are also in charge of the excellent Dead River Area Historical Society Museum across the street, which is closed in the winter; 207-246-6901 or 800-943-6995.

Three Stanley Avenue is an antique-furnished Victorian home on a side street in Kingfield. Rates are very reasonable and include breakfast served at their restaurant next door; 207-265-5541.

DINING

Seasons is the restaurant in The Sugarloaf Inn at the base of the mountain. In a bright, window-lined atmosphere, this is much, much more than a *ho-hum-let's-eat-here-because-it's-handy* resort dining room. We've never had anything less than exceptional dinners at Seasons, where the menu is innovative and the ingredients are fresh and chosen from New England's bounty. The presentation is impeccable and fresh herbs are used to complement the flavors, not hide the meal. Vegetables are treated with respect; in fact one delicious entree is their roasted vegetable cassoulet, a melange of baby squash, beets, white beans, shiitake mushrooms, grilled Roma tomatoes and fresh rosemary. We liked the wild game board as an appetizer, since it gave us a chance to sample three different pate varieties. For a real treat, give the chef carte blanche with your entree and try his spontaneous creation of the day. Each evening, one special is priced under $10; 207-237-6834.

Although it's a close call based on many factors, our personal favorite in the area is **The Porter House** in Eustis, north of Carrabassett Valley. Beth and Jeff Hinman have resisted the temptation to crowd in a extra table here and there, in order to keep the small rooms of this village house uncrowded. Good service, a genial atmosphere, and outstanding food nicely presented have made this chef-owned restaurant popular with people from both Rangeley and Sugarloaf who don't mind driving to get there. Careful attention to details is the key: each salad seems to have been personally designed by the chef and the almond-crusted duck strips with chutney has to be the best starter in the state, although stuffed mushrooms and a house pate are also right up there. Lobster Brittany is perfectly seasoned and the pairing of meat, vegetables and sauces is flawless. And a very good wine list with quite reasonable prices doesn't hurt, either. They are open for dinner every day except Christmas. Do reserve ahead, since they won't hurry someone out to make room for you; 207-246-7932.

One Stanley Avenue is often listed among the state's best restaurants, right along with the bastions of fine dining in the posh coastal resort towns. The menu uses fresh local ingredients, especially those which are indigenous to Maine, such as fiddleheads, wild blueberries, apple cider, salmon and maple products. Veal and fiddlehead pie is one of the favorites here, and although its atmosphere is fairly formal, you don't need to be: your turtleneck and sweater will be right at home here. As in a fine restaurant anywhere, expect to pay more than steak-and-fries prices; 207-265-5541.

Tufulio's offers Italian specialties and steaks, chicken and seafood, in informal surroundings with oak booths. They usually have a two-for-one dinner on Sundays; 207-235-2010.

Mainely Yours on Route 27 in Stratton is the local gathering place for breakfast and lunch; a clothesline strung over the counter is the community bulletin board, although we suspect word passes quickly enough without it. It opens at 5 a.m. Monday through Friday, at 6 a.m. on Saturday, and 7:30 a.m. on Sundays Weekend breakfasts are all you can eat for $4.95.

White Wolf in Stratton serves hearty wild game dishes and a general menu in a rustic setting, offering two-for-one dinners on Tuesday and Wednesday evenings. They also serve breakfast starting at 7 a.m.; 207-246-2922.

For a good breakfast, look hard in the back of **Anni's Market** for the few tables tucked among the merchandise.

INDEX